Acquiring and Organizing Curriculum Materials

Gary A. Lare

The Scarecrow Press, Inc.
Lanham, Md., & London 1997

SCARECROW PRESS, INC.

Published in the United States of America
by Scarecrow Press, Inc.
4720 Boston Way
Lanham, Maryland 20706

British Library Cataloguing in Publication Information Available

Library of Congress Cataloging-in-Publication Data

Lare, Gary.
     Acquiring and organizing curriculum materials / Gary A. Lare.
        p.   cm.
     Includes bibliographical references and index.
     ISBN 0-8108-3347-6 (pbk. : alk. paper)
     1. Instructional materials centers—Collection development—
United States.   2. Education libraries—Collection development—
United States.   3. Media programs (Education)—United States.
4. Curriculum planning—United States.   I. Title.
LB3044.72.L37   1997
027.7—dc21   97-17597
                                                                              CIP

ISBN 0-8108-3347-6 (pbk. : alk. paper)

To my wife,
Martha

to my children,
Kevin and Kathleen

Contents

Preface

The purpose of this book is to address two important questions for a curriculum materials center: where to find curriculum materials for acquisition and how to organize these materials for efficient and effective access once they are acquired. The various types of curriculum materials are not readily and conveniently listed in a basic reference tool such as *Books in Print*. One must search out these materials (curriculum guides, textbooks, teaching activities books, audiovisual media/instructional materials) in various catalogs and brochures. Many excellent sources of curriculum materials are missed because they have not come to the attention of the busy curriculum materials librarian or are not indexed in a useful way.

This book brings together many companies, associations, projects, and government agencies that publish, produce, and distribute curriculum materials. In addition, it lists materials by curriculum subject area and material format. Curriculum librarians are thus provided with a comprehensive tool for collection development and an important reference regarding sources of curriculum materials. The book should also prove to be useful to school library media specialists who acquire many of the types of materials covered in the book. Even though many curriculum materials centers (CMCs) have children and young adult books in their collections, these types of materials were not considered for this book because their acquisition is more straightforward than the acquisition of other curriculum materials.

In addition to the materials that can be purchased for the collection, it is useful for curriculum librarians to have a listing of Internet sites that contain curriculum materials. Included in this book is a large list of World Wide Web sites and links that provide teaching activities and lesson plans, curriculum guides and standards, and curriculum resource links that provide content to support lesson plans.

A curriculum materials collection should have not only the types of materials listed above but also professional-level reference and resource books that support the various areas of the collection. Such professional materials include books on media and technology, instructional materials reviews, bibliographies of curriculum guides, and textbook reviews. A recommended list of these types of works is provided.

Once curriculum materials are acquired, they must be organized in such a way that they can be easily accessed. Because of the special nature of curriculum materials, certain problems must be solved. Various shelving options and classification schemes are presented so that informed decisions can be made regarding how to organize the various collections.

Part I

Acquiring and Organizing the Collection

Chapter One

Curriculum Guides: Acquiring the Collection

This chapter deals with the many and varied resources collected by a curriculum materials center called "curriculum publications" or "curriculum documents." They are procured from many different sources and usually fall into the categories of curriculum guides, courses of study, unit and lesson plans, and curriculum bulletins and reports. Many CMC directors use some of these terms interchangeably. However, there is a difference and a distinction that needs to be made, at least intellectually, as each type serves a particular purpose in its contribution to the curriculum.

A *course of study* is general in nature and broadly defines the educational program in terms of philosophy, goals, and objectives. Leo H. Bradley points out that the course of study "is the official statement of what shall be taught in the classrooms of a school district."[1] A course of study basically prescribes what is to be taught in a particular subject or area of concentration in a given grade or combination of grades. It is usually mandated by state law that school districts develop and implement these documents. Most state departments of education have developed curriculum "frameworks" to help guide school districts in their development of courses of study. As Allan A. Glatthorn states "some of those frameworks are very general, specifying only goals and graduation requirements: others are more specific and thus more constraining."[2]

A *curriculum guide* is suggestive in nature as it gives ideas on how a subject or area of study might be taught. It is specific in comparison to a course of study. According to Glatthorn, a curriculum guide could include such components as the district's educational goals, subject mastery goals, curriculum framework for the subject, a scope-and-sequence chart, the grade-level objectives, recommended time allocations, recommended sequence for teaching objectives, recommended teaching activities for each objective, recommended means of assessing student learning, and a list of textbooks and resources.[3]

A *curriculum bulletin* or report provides information on a particular focus area. These documents provide school personnel with background information to develop and implement curricular programs. Examples of titles in this category are: *Creating an Environment for Learning Disabilities: A Resource and Planning Guide*, *Read from the Start*, *Community Education*, *Gifted Education Resource Directory*, *School Science Laboratories: A Guide to Some Hazardous Substances*. Curriculum bulletins are most prevalently produced by state departments of education.

Collection Development

Every curriculum materials center needs to have a collection of curriculum guides (for simplicity, the term "curriculum guides" will be used as a generic term for the rest of this chapter to refer to courses of study, frameworks, curriculum bulletins and reports, as well as actual curriculum guides). Furthermore, this collection should have all of the above types of curriculum publications represented so that the various needs associated with each type can be met. Curriculum materials centers, however, vary in the breadth and depth with which they collect curriculum guides. Some rely totally on the Kraus Curriculum Development Library on microfiche (to be described later). Others supplement the microfiche with paper copies, particularly local and state publications. Still others collect only paper copies. How many curriculum guides a given CMC collects will depend upon local needs, but a basic collection needs to be available. The collection should have a good representation of curriculum guides from across the nation, both from state departments as well as from school districts. This writer chaired a committee established by the Curriculum Materials Interest Group of the Academic Library Association of Ohio whose focus was to develop guidelines for curriculum materials centers to follow. This committee's work is described more fully in chapter 3. The *Guidelines for Curriculum Materials Centers* can be found in the appendix. The guidelines established for collection development in the area of curriculum guides are:

a. These guides shall reflect those used in the institution's region as well as a representative collection from other areas.
b. Major areas of the curriculum shall be represented with the scope reflecting the certification programs of the education unit at the institution.
c. These guides shall reflect current trends in education and be acquired annually.[4]

Regarding collection quantities, the *Guidelines* states that there should be a minimum of 0.5 titles for each full-time equivalent education student.[5]

The collection development policy for the Curriculum Resources Laboratory (CRL) at the University of Iowa substantiates the idea that the curriculum guide collection can be somewhat ecclectic. It states: "*Scope*: The Curriculum Guide Collection includes Preschool–Grade 12 guides from school districts and state departments of education. . . . Occasionally, professional materials that are donated to the CRL that do not fit elsewhere in the collection are housed here as well."[6]

As stated above, the collection should represent a cross section of guides produced across the country. This will maintain variety in the collection and provide various viewpoints to compare and contrast. Often graduate courses in curriculum development in the various disciplines and local school personnel need a variety of materials to study. In addition, undergraduates often use these resources to gather ideas for formulating lesson plans. It is also important to have a more comprehensive collection of state and local curriculum guides because these are probably in much demand for certain assignments, and in particular, for those preparing for field experiences in the local schools.

Usually this mix of representative curriculum guides from across the country and a more comprehensive collection of local guides seems to meet most teacher education programmatic needs. This selection plan is represented in the University of Iowa CRL plan which states: "Preschool through twelfth-grade curriculum guides from state departments of education and from public school systems are purchased selectively."[7] Furthermore, along this same line, the collection development policy for the Curriculum Materials Center at Moorhead State University, Minnesota, states: "Curriculum bulletins for preschool through twelfth grade are included. Bulletins published by the Minnesota Department of Education are collected comprehensively, while bulletins from other states, districts, or special agencies are collected selectively."[8]

As stated earlier, many CMCs purchase the Kraus Curriculum Development Library on microfiche. This collection is wonderful in that it has a variety of curriculum publications which are published by state departments of education and various school districts across the country as well as professional organizations. Access is provided by a paper index which permits one to find curriculum guides by subject as well as a CD-ROM which provides further indexing. This microfiche collection is of particular value to curriculum developers and graduate students conducting research. It is also of use to preservice teachers who are searching for curriculum standards, objectives, and lesson plan ideas.

All CMCs, however, should have a reasonable collection of paper curriculum guides available regardless of whether the CMC owns the Kraus Curriculum Development Library or not. Many preservice teachers prefer the quick availability of paper copies of curriculum guides. With a good classification system, guides for a particular curriculum area can be grouped together and readily available for quick browsing. Paper copies also mean that they can be easily checked out and used at the student's convenience away from the CMC. Furthermore, photocopying of a particular section can be quickly carried out from paper copies. However, paper copies take up more shelf space and require more maintenance. In addition, collecting paper copies of curriculum guides does mean more time in selection, but it is time well worth spending.

Curriculum Guide Collection Acquisition

The first step in selecting curriculum guides is to ascertain the addresses of curriculum guide publication sources. To get a wide range of curriculum guides, it is recommended that all state departments of education be contacted. In addition, major school systems across the country should be solicited. Addresses of state departments of education and school systems can be procured from various reference sources. Once a list of possible sources has been compiled, a letter should be drafted and sent to each agency on your list inquiring about the availability of curriculum guides either free or for a price. If you are starting from scratch or with a very small paper copy collection, you will want to do some retrospective procurement. You will be able to acquire curriculum guides that are as much as six to eight years old. If, however, you have a fairly good-sized collection, it is important to acquire the most recent publications so that your collection is as current as possible. This will mean that your collection will reflect many of the newer trends in curriculum that continually occur. Below is a sample letter that could be sent to request newer materials.

It can be noted that the request is for a list of available curriculum guides that displays the dates of publication. This is very important if one wants to purchase recent curriculum guides to update the collection. It has been found, however, that many schools and departments of education do not list the publication dates on their availability lists. Once the letters are sent and replies are received, you may find that some sources contacted do not provide curriculum guides even for a price; others have not published any recently; still others will provide guides free of charge or for price.

A good cycle to follow in soliciting curriculum guides to up-

---

To Whom It May Concern:

The Curriculum Materials Center at the University of _____ is in the process of updating its curriculum guide/course of study collection. We would very much like to see your curriculum guides represented on our shelves. Please send me a list and prices, if applicable, of the curriculum guides that you have produced since _____. A total list of your available curriculum guides would also be useful if it shows publication dates. In addition, *if you have any curriculum publications (produced in the last three years) that you can send at no charge*, this would be very much appreciated.

Thank you for considering my request. You will be contributing to the knowledge and development of many preservice and inservice teachers.

Please mail your list and/or publications to:

Sincerely,

date a collection is every two years. The process of curriculum guide development is a long process, and sending a request every two years gives agencies time to develop new guides since the last time you inquired. However, as the guideline above suggests, curriculum guides should be added to the collection annually. In the years between comprehensive soliciting, one can select from lists and other sources listed below or new publications from professional associations. See chapter 9 for a selected list of state departments of education and school systems that provide lists of available curriculum publications.

In addition to sending letters of request to state departments of education and school systems, another useful selection tool is the annual publication of the Association for Supervision and Curriculum Development, *Curriculum Materials Directory*. This publication lists and describes curriculum publications displayed at the annual conference of the Association for Supervision and Curriculum Development. This is useful, as are the lists obtained from various state departments of education and schools, for filling in the collection where gaps in coverage occur as well as to find newer guides to add to the collection.

Another fine selection source for language arts curriculum guides is *Commended English Language Arts Curriculum Guides, K–12*, published by the National Council of Teachers of English. This useful publication lists recommended curriculum guides with annotations. A similar publication entitled *Exemplary Art Curricula: A Guide to Guides* is available from the National Art Education Association. This book details twenty-six criteria for evaluating art guides with examples of the criteria from actual guides. Of particular interest are the addresses of the sources of the various guides cited.

In addition to the above sources, it is a good idea to keep your catalogs current for the various professional associations representing different curricular disciplines. These organizations periodically publish curriculum guides. Of particular importance are the curriculum standards produced by these associations which state the recommended course for the school curriculums to take for their discipline. In addition to the professional associations, grants are often given to various agencies by the U.S. Department of Education to develop curriculum documents such as standards.

The curriculum materials center should have a supporting collection of professional education resources that support the curriculum guide collection and provide standards and curriculum guidelines, as well as resources such as those mentioned above that list available curriculum guides. A list of these resources is provided in chapter 8.

The Kraus Curriculum Development Library (KCDL) mentioned above is currently, as of this writing, only on microfiche. Presently, KCDL annually publishes approximately 300 curriculum guides. These guides are collected from state departments of education, school districts from all over the United States, and professional organizations. Kraus applies particular criteria in evaluating the curriculum guides received. Those that meet the standards are then selected for inclusion. The collection may be procured from:

Kraus Curriculum Development Library
4611-F Assembly Dr.
Lanham, MD 20706–4391

The ERIC microfiche collection is another source for curriculum guides. Many CMCs, however, do not have the fiche collection in their facility, as it is often housed with the rest of the library's microfiche collection. Regardless of where the ERIC microfiche collection is housed, as long as it is accessible to your CMC users it will be a good supplement to your CMC collection. ERIC is particularly useful in locating curriculum guides that you need to fill in gaps in coverage in the CMC paper collection. This is easily done by conducting a search on ERIC for guides in the area(s) that you need. In an automated search, simply enter the curriculum subject along with the publication type, 052, and a list of available guides will be produced. Once suitable guides have been found, then paper copies can be reproduced by ERIC's Document Reproduction Service (EDRS), (800-443-ERIC).

Notes

1. Leo H. Bradley, *Curriculum Leadership and Development Handbook* (Englewood Cliffs, NJ: Prentice-Hall, 1985), 43.
2. Allan A. Glatthorn, *Developing a Quality Curriculum* (Alexandria, VA: Association for Supervision and Curriculum Development, 1994), 36–37).
3. Glatthorn, *Developing a Quality Curriculum*, 44.
4. *Guidelines for Curriculum Materials Centers* (Cincinnati, OH: Academic Library Association Curriculum Materials Centers Interest Group, 1992), 3.
5. *Guidelines for Curriculum Materials Centers*, 8.

6. *Collection Development Policy: Curriculum Resources Laboratory* (Iowa City, IA: University of Iowa, 1993).

7. *Collection Development Policy: Curriculum Resources Laboratory.*

8. *Collection Development Policy: Curriculum Materials Center* (Moorhead, MN: Moorhead State University, n.d.), 26.

Chapter Two

Curriculum Guides: Organizing the Collection

There are basically two ways that the curriculum guide collection can be arranged for access by CMC users. The guides can be placed in filing cabinets or arranged on shelves. There are various possible shelving arrangements. For example, the guides can be shelved separately from the other formats, e.g., textbooks and teaching activity books, or intershelved with all of these various formats, or any other combination. In practice, it seems that there are two overall usage patterns in desiring access to curriculum materials such as curriculum guides, textbooks, and teaching activities books. One pattern is that student assignments and user reference questions are directed toward one particular format, e.g., textbooks or curriculum guides or teaching activity books. At times, however, users follow a second usage pattern and are simply looking for curriculum content and lesson plan ideas and will want to look at a variety of formats. Therefore, by separating the curriculum guides from the other formats, the former usage pattern is accommodated by having the curriculum guides all together in one place. However, when this shelving arrangement is employed, the user must search in more places to satisfy the second usage pattern. If the curriculum guides are interfiled with textbooks, etc., the second usage pattern is well accommodated because all formats are together under the same subject. With this intershelving arrangement, however, in order to satisfy the former usage pattern of looking for a particular format, the format must appear prominently on the material, most likely in the call number.

Some CMCs prefer to shelve curriculum guides separately from textbooks and teaching activity books. For elementary school-level subjects, there will be a general subject classification number given to the curriculum guide or textbook series. However, users planning lessons will be needing materials on specific concepts or skills, e.g., simple machines or tropical rain forests. Even if the formats are intershelved, the users will still have to look through each of these formats to find their material. By having the various formats shelved separately, not only does it make it convenient for users desiring one format to easily find what they are looking for and work with the materials, but it helps the user planning a lesson to concentrate or focus the lesson planning process. This involves first going to the curriculum guide shelving area to locate an objective(s) for the lesson being planned. Granted, the curriculum guide (as a type of curriculum publication discussed earlier), as opposed to most courses of study, could also have suggested teaching activities and resources and these could be noted. The main idea, though, is to gather information as to what is taught, with appropriate objectives, in a particular grade level with appropriate sequencing. The curriculum guide functions very nicely for this purpose. Next, the user in the lesson planning process would go to the teaching activity book section of the CMC. By being separated from other formats, all books dealing with teaching activities can be easily browsed by the user for ideas. Specific teaching activities would be sought out to use with the concept(s) and objective(s) found in the curriculum guides. Finally, instructional materials would be searched for to incorporate in the lesson. This would mean going to the textbook section as well as the audiovisual media to search for materials to use with the students for which the lesson is being planned. Added suggestions could also be picked up from the teacher's editions of textbooks to use in the lesson plan.

In addition to providing access as discussed above, having the formats separated, particularly the curriculum guides from the textbooks, helps to address a curricular concern. The textbook as a format is a teaching resource; it is not a course of study or even a curriculum guide in the purist sense. Too often the textbook becomes a curriculum guide in and of itself for the teacher instead of support material, along with other teaching resources such as audiovisual media, for an overriding course of study. By separating curriculum guides and textbooks on the shelf, a subtle statement is made that they are not synonomous types of materials.

Since most curriculum guides are paperback, some CMCs find it easier to file them in filing cabinets. Also, many CMCs, or at least their cataloging centers, consider curriculum guides to be ephemeral and not worth the time of cataloging. Contributing to this decision not to catalog is the fact that many curriculum guides do not have copy cataloging in OCLC, which means more staff time in original cataloging. Carol Wilson points out that not including curriculum materials in general "in an institution's automation plans in a timely manner will lead to user problems, perpetuate expensive labor-intensive manual systems, and hinder resource sharing."[1] It is very important that curriculum guides be entered in the catalog, either card or OPAC, so that bibliographic accessibility to these excellent resources is made possible. In addition, an OPAC system with barcoded curriculum guides makes circulation of this format a breeze.

There are various ways that a drawer-filed curriculum guide can be labeled. One method is to assign a broad curriculum area on the first line (which allows for filing alphabetically by subject), the publisher on the second line, and the grade level(s) on the third line.

Mathematics	Science
Hudson City Schools	Ohio Dept. of Education
K–12	5–6

Another method is to follow the above scheme but to add a classification number on the line after the alpha subject. In this case the class number is from the LT schedule (explained in chapter 4 on textbook organization).

ART	MATH
2000	4400
Brown County Bd of Education	Brown County Bd of Education
K–12	7–12

The guides are then placed in folders which are labeled with the broad curriculum area.

A preferred way that many CMCs arrange curriculum guides is to place them on shelves. This is especially useful because many of these guides are just too thick for easy filing in a filing cabinet. Also, by being arranged on the shelf by a classification number means that this format will be accessed like the other curriculum materials in the collection. The problem of their being mostly paperback means that they will not have a lot of stability for standing up on the shelf, however. One way that this can be remedied is to purchase pamphlet boxes to house the curriculum guides on the shelf. An additional touch is to purchase colored plastic pamphlet boxes. Various colors could be used to represent the broad curriculum areas, e.g., red for language arts, green for science, blue for social studies. Even though individual guides have class numbers on them, this system of colors helps students quickly find curriculum guides in a particular discipline. Another way to stabilize the curriculum guides which has been used successfully by this writer is to send the curriculum guides out to the commercial bindery that your library uses and have the guides bound with economy binding. Similar to the pamphlet boxes above, various colors of binding can be chosen to represent the broad curriculum areas that the curriculum guides represent, e.g., blue for social studies, maroon for art, yellow for mathematics. An even less expensive binding than the economy type that can be used is mylar. This type of binding, however, eliminates the ability to use colored bindings to represent curriculum areas.

Classification/Call Number Considerations

It is important that five items appear in the call numbers of curriculum guides. The subject should be present in either alpha or numeric form, which will place all curriculum guides for a given curriculum area together. Of particular value is that the subject designator go beyond just the broad curriculum area. For example, social studies (if not general elementary) would be subdivided into at least the areas of history, geography, political science, economics, etc. A second item needed is the publishing body, whether it is school system, state department of education, or commercial. This makes the location of particular sources of curriculum guides readily accessible within the given subject. The third item needed in the call number is the grade level covered by the guide. It is also important that the publication year be present. This places a timeframe in the mind of the user very quickly upon looking at the call number on the shelf. Finally, whether the curriculum guides are shelved as a separate collection or intershelved with other formats, there should be some designation made for the curriculum guide format. As in textbooks, the call number items should be as simplified as possible and make sense without a lot of interpretation.

Below are some actual classification/call number schemes being used by CMCs: Library of Congress, Dewey Decimal, and other systems. Not all of these schemes display all five recommended items for a call number, however.

Library of Congress Classification Scheme (modified)

Subject:	PC	speech
Grade level:	E	secondary level
Issuing body: (state/city)	PEN/PIT	Pennsylvania/Pittsburgh

Subject:	HF	business math
Grade level:	E	secondary level
Issuing body: (state/city)	ARZ/PHO	Arizona/Phoenix

Subject:	PB	developmental reading
Grade level:	A	all grades
Issuing body:	ILL	Illinois State Department of Education
(state/city)		

Subject:	PA3	spelling
Grade level:	1-3	first through third grades
Issuing body: (state/city)	CAL/LOS	California/Los Angeles

Grade level designations used in this scheme (if just one grade or a few grades, these are noted as numbers):

A: all grades
B: kindergarten
C: elementary school
D: junior high school
E: secondary school

Dewey Decimal Classification Scheme

Two different Dewey Decimal classification schemes are presented below.

Example 1

In this first scheme, the broad grade-level designations are:

all—370.7   special—371.9   early—372.21
elementary—372.24   secondary—373.07   adult—374.0

Broad grade level:	372.24	elementary
Subject/format:	5003	science(500)/curriculum guide(3)
LC state cutter:	T4	Texas
School district cutter:	H537	Highland Park

Broad grade level:	370.7	all grades
Subject/format:	5103	math(510)/curriculum guide(3)
LC state cutter:	O3m	Ohio Dept. of Education

Broad grade level:	373.07	secondary
Subject/format:	5103	math(510)/curriculum guide(3)
LC state cutter:	W4	West Virginia Dept. of Education
	4	volume 4 in series

Broad grade level:	372.24	elementary
Subject/format:	7803	music(780)/curriculum guide(3)
LC state cutter:	T4	Texas
School district cutter:	H537	Highland Park
	2	volume 2 (second grade)

This classification scheme is further elaborated upon in chapter 4 on textbook organization.

Example 2

Format:	CUR GDE	curriculum guide
Subject code:	512	algebra
Issuing body (4 letters):	SPRI	Springfield (MO) schools
Year of publication:	1995	publication year
Grade level:	Gr 9–12	grades 9–12

Format:	CUR GDE	curriculum guide
Subject code:	468	Spanish
Issuing body:	CHUH	Cleveland Heights/ University Heights
Year of publication:	1990	publication year
Grade level:	Gr 9–12	grades 9–12

Format:	CUR GDE	curriculum guide
Subject code:	300	social studies
Issuing body:	ALSDE	Alabama State Dept. Of Education
Year of publication:	1992	publication year
Grade level:	Gr K–12	grades kindergarten through 12

Format:	CUR GDE	curriculum guide
Subject code:	500	science
Issuing body:	CHIC	Chicago City Schools
Year of publication:	1994	publication year
Grade level:	Gr 1	grade one

This classification scheme is listed in chapter 4 on textbook organization. Curriculum guides containing more than one subject in the same book are classified in the following way: elementary (372.19); secondary (373.19); K–12 (375). Curriculum design/evaluation guides are classed 375.001.

Other Local Classification Schemes

The next two classification schemes are examples of locally designed plans.

Example 1

Subject (alpha)-subcategory (numeric):	MA-3	mathematics-algebra
Publisher/year of publication:	ORLA/96	Orlando Schools/1996
Grade level(s):	S	senior high school
Format:	CG	curriculum guide

Subject (alpha)-subcategory (numeric):	LA-7	language arts-spelling
Publisher/year of publication:	CA/94	California Dept. of Education/1994
Grade level(s):	E	elementary school
Format:	CG	curriculum guide

Subject (alpha)-subcategory (numeric):	SS-1	social studies-basic
Publisher/year of publication:	PITT/92	Pittsburgh Schools
Grade level(s):	1–3	first through third grades
Format:	CG	curriculum guide

The complete schedule the above were taken from is listed in chapter 4 on textbook organization.

Example 2

Format.subject (alpha):	C. So	curriculum guide—social studies
State cutter (2 places):	I64	Iowa
Issuing body cutter (2 places) plus workmark for title:	C38s	Cedar Rapids Community Schools (*Supplementary Activities to be used . . .*)
Format.subject (alpha):	C. So	curriculum guide social studies
State cutter (2 places):	C15	California
Issuing body cutter (2 places) plus workmark for title:	S79s	State Dept. of Education (*Social Science Framework*)

As shown above, there are a variety of ways to organize the curriculum guide collection. It is important that a meaningful plan be adopted and consistently followed. Curriculum guides are important resource materials in lesson planning and curriculum development and must be organized for access with the same attention to detail that is used with other types of curriculum materials.

Notes

1. Carole F. Wilson, Mary M. Finley, and Alice S. Clark, "Cataloging Practices and Resource Sharing of Curriculum Collections in Academic Libraries," *Journal of Library Administration* 6, no. 4 (Winter 1985/86): 82.

Chapter Three

K–12 Textbooks: Acquiring the Collection

As in all areas of collection development for the CMC, when it comes to the textbook area some basic questions must be answered: what curriculum areas should be covered (scope); how many textbooks do we need in a given area; which titles should be added; and what edition types (workbooks, teacher's editions, resource books, etc.) are needed?

Many times, funding drives the size, scope, and currency of the textbook collection rather than curricular and instructional needs. Enough funding must be found so that this collection can hold its own relative position in meeting needs along with other areas in the educational book collection, such as curriculum theory, instructional methodology, education history and philosophy, etc. It seems that many CMCs must limp along and depend on donations to provide preK–12 textbooks for the collection. Textbooks as instructional materials are changing as they reflect interactive technology; more and more textbooks are being published with computer programs, CD-ROMs, and videodiscs to accompany the printed materials. Some states have even adopted a series of videodiscs with accompanying curriculum materials as a "textbook" option. All of these features are reflected in a higher purchase price. The faces of textbooks often change also to reflect various current instructional approaches. For example, basal reading or literacy books have changed their materials to accommodate the whole language approach to developing literacy skills. Now these series include trade book titles, big books, cassettes, etc. However, the printed textbook is still viable today and is being used in the schools. The CMC must find the funding necessary to meet textbook needs in a proactive collection-developing posture, not relying just on gifts.

What curriculum areas should be represented in the CMC collection? A basic way this can be determined is to collect only in those curriculum fields that are certification areas in your education program. For example, if your department or college of education does not have a certification program in vocational or business education, then textbooks representing these areas are not collected. CMCs located in states which have textbook adoption lists collect only the state adopted textbooks, regardless whether the books represent certification areas at their institutions or not. This method can result in seldom used textbooks that do not reflect institutional certification areas occupying valuable shelf space. If the adopted textbooks are donated by the state, there is no problem with funding for the CMC. However, this approach can become somewhat costly if all of these state-adopted books are purchased by the CMC. Some CMCs in states with state adoption plans collect comprehensively those textbooks that are selected from the list for adoption by local school districts and collect more selectively those from the state list that are not adopted locally. Other CMCs in states that do not adopt textbooks often collect textbooks in their certification curriculum areas but purchase only those textbook titles that have been adopted by local school districts.

The textbook collection should not be limited to a list of adopted books. For one reason, although state lists are relatively easy to obtain as decisions are made and the state curriculum area adoption cycle is known, it is very difficult to keep up with the various adoption patterns of the different local school districts near the CMC. Also, if one only collects textbooks once they are adopted, there is the possibility, because of time lags in this adoption process, that the CMC would not be purchasing many of the textbooks just published. Therefore, the important goal of having materials in the collection that reflect the latest in curriculum and instructional approaches would often be unrealized. This is not to say that attempts should not be made to obtain copies of locally adopted textbooks, as these are often needed for field experiences and other assignments. However, just limiting textbook collection development to these books will result in an inadequate collection.

A better approach to maintaining balance in the textbook collection, both from the standpoint of having adopted textbooks to meet students' field experience needs and other assignments, as well as to provide the latest published textbook examples of educational approaches and emphases, is to acquire as many of the newly published textbooks each year as is possible. Due to funding limitations, such purchases may have to be limited to just teacher's annotated editions. This approach also is made easier if comprehensive purchases are made in curriculum certification programs that have the greatest number of students, and more selective decisions are made in areas where not as many students are enrolled. Of course, no acquisition is made of textbooks in curriculum areas that are not represented by certification programs in the CMC's institutional education program. This approach in textbook collection development has become easier in recent years, as fewer and fewer textbook companies exist because of mergers.

The University of Iowa Curriculum Resources Laboratory (CRL) follows the above approach of trying to obtain as many textbooks in general, but particularly those in heavily used areas. Its collection development policy reads:

> Textbooks in most K–12 curricular areas will be requested from the major publishers. The CRL attempts to obtain at least the teacher's edition of a particular book or series. Highest priority will be given to obtaining texts in language arts, reading, social studies, math, and science. Few, if any, textbooks will be collected in areas that are not taught in the COE [College of Education] (ex. home ec [economics] education or industrial arts).[1]

The Curriculum Resources Center at the University of Cincinnati comprehensively collects textbooks in the curriculum areas of language arts, social studies, science, and mathematics because of the heavy use while being more selective in the less used areas of art, music, health, and foreign languages. No collection development efforts are made in the areas of business education, industrial arts, vocational education, home economics, and physical education as these areas are not certification fields at the University. A combination approach of collecting locally used texts, as well as those that are not necessarily adopted locally, is used by the Curriculum Materials Center at Moorhead University in Minnesota. Its collection development policy states: "Textbooks include all curricular subjects, grades kindergarten through twelve. Textbooks adopted by local school districts are normally acquired, while other exemplary texts, particularly those recommended by instructors or methods courses, are collected selectively."[2] These CMCs are typical in that textbooks are collected for preschool through grade 12 only and do not include college textbooks.

The Curriculum Materials Center Interest Group (CMCIG) of

the Academic Library Association of Ohio is an organization whose members are the CMC directors from colleges and universities throughout Ohio. A committee of this group developed *Guidelines for Curriculum Materials Centers*, which was approved by the CMCIG members. The complete *Guidelines* can be found in the appendix.

Relative to the textbook collection, the *Guidelines* states that:

a. This collection shall reflect the texts used in the public schools in the region and schools in which the teacher education students receive field placements.[3]

The *Guidelines* intends that the collection should not be necessarily limited to the textbooks used in the regional schools by the following guidelines:

b. Several publishers shall be represented for each grade level in the major curriculum areas, including English, social studies, language arts, science, mathematics, music, art, health, modern languages, and vocational education. The scope of curriculum areas varies, however, according to the certification programs of the education unit at the institution.

c. The collection shall be updated annually, reflecting new curriculum emphases and patterns.[4]

In summary, gifts and donations should not be the driving force for developing this collection. Instead, it should reflect textbooks used in local schools where education students receive practicum or field placements. In addition (and not necessarily mutually exclusive of the textbooks used locally), the collection must contain recently published textbooks that reflect current trends in curriculum and instructional approaches. It is further recommended that in order to keep the collection reflecting current educational practices no textbook, unless a particular need exists, be kept longer than ten years. With limited funds, more efforts can be placed in obtaining more textbooks for those certification fields in the educational program that are most heavily used and less for those areas where enrollments are not as great. This does not mean, however, that exemplary textbooks will not be purchased for these lesser-enrolled programs. No textbooks need be purchased for curriculum areas that do not have certification programs at the CMC's institution. Regarding quantity of textbooks in the CMC collection, the *Guidelines for Curriculum Ma-*

terials Centers mentioned above recommends a minimum of five titles for each full-time equivalent teacher education student.[5]

As for collection development, it is important that the CMC develops a plan to follow in textbook acquisition (as well as for other CMC materials) and that the plan be written down in the form of a collection development policy. A good model to help in developing a collection development policy can be found in the ALA publication, *Curriculum Materials Center Collection Development Policy.*[6] This volume details the areas and issues to be covered in the policy as well as providing sample wording.

Textbook Collection Acquisition

As in all areas of the CMC collection, textbooks are added annually to the collection. An essential acquisition tool for acquiring textbooks is the current catalogs of textbook publishers. It has been found in practice that very few textbook publishers will place a CMC on a mailing list to receive the current catalog on an annual basis. Therefore, these publishers must be contacted each year for their latest catalog.

One facet of the acquisition process is to add those textbooks that have been recently adopted by local schools. As stated before, keeping up with the various school district's adoption decisions is often very time-consuming, particularly if education students are placed in many different districts. The task is made somewhat easier if the majority of the students tend to be placed in just a few districts. The adopted books in only those districts would therefore be targeted for acquisition. Nevertheless, with decisions being made at various times by curriculum committees in different curriculum areas, it often takes a lot of contacts with the districts to keep apprised. Once lists of the adopted titles have been obtained, it is just a matter of consulting the latest catalog from the given publisher to find ordering information and to determine what edition types to obtain (e.g., student's text, teacher's edition, student workbook).

One approach to obtaining copies of the books is to approach the publishers' sales representatives in the hope that some titles will be donated to you. However, the days of CMC gift copies of textbooks from publishers have basically come and gone. Sometimes one will find a representative willing to do this, but it is usually rare. One publisher, D.C. Heath, will give discounts to education professors who wish to have Heath textbooks placed in their curriculum libraries. A better approach is to request that faculty who teach methods courses ask publishers in the exhibit area of professional conferences they attend for examination copies of textbooks to use with their classes. Once the faculty member has used the books with his or her classes, they can be given to the CMC. Another effective method for those CMCs located in a textbook nonadoption state is to contact local school districts that have been reviewing textbooks for adoption. The schools are often looking for a place to donate those textbooks reviewed but not chosen. Of course, this method does not result in acquiring adopted texts, but does permit one to receive some excellent books. As stated before, however, the collection will be very ineffective if it is built only with gifts. Unless, the CMC is a depository for state-adopted textbooks, funds will have to be expended.

As the *Guidelines* states, the textbook collection shall be updated annually so that new curriculum emphases and patterns are reflected. Therefore, a second facet of textbook acquisition is to obtain currently published books which may be available before a particular curriculum area comes up in the school districts' or state adoption cycles. Again, it is important to have current publishers' catalogs to keep informed of what is available. A schedule that works very well is to request the catalogs in the fall of the academic year, usually around early November. By then the publishers have printed their catalogs for books being published with the following calendar year's copyright date, as well as earlier editions. By the time the catalogs arrive and the new books are chosen, ordered, cataloged, and placed on the shelf, the new calendar year will have commenced and the books will be very current.

A third facet of textbook collection development is to evaluate the collection for weaknesses. For example, the collection may be weak in secondary literature books, or supplementary social studies books about minorities, or possibly English as a Second Language (ESL) books. A great acquisition tool for filling in the textbook collection or for finding a requested title is *EL-HI Textbooks & Serials in Print*. This book allows one to search by curriculum area, title, series or author. Another set of resources for locating textbooks are the *Brown's Directories of Instructional Programs*. These books, listed in chapter 8, go a step further than the *El-Hi Textbooks* in that the textbooks are narratively described. No evaluations are given, however. Each volume in this series covers a major curriculum area for either the secondary or elementary grades. None of these resources, however, lists publishers that produce a particular type of textbook material, either by subject, grade level, or type of material, such as supplementary, videodisc interactive, etc. Such listings are provided in chapters 10, 11, and 12. Having this type of information and the current catalog of the publisher listed will greatly support acquisitions efforts. These lists will also aid in reference assistance with CMC users. For example, clientele may wish to find secondary-level high interest/low readability textbooks in the area of social studies, or perhaps there is a need to find publishers of literature books with accompanying audiocassettes of the selections. There may also be a desire to find science textbooks that have supporting videodiscs with barcode access, etc. These lists are also good sources for the CMC director to use to produce a list of textbook publishers from which catalogs can be procured and then placed in the CMC publishers' catalog file which is maintained for public access.

There is a growing number of textbook information being provided on the Internet. A list of World Wide Web textbook publisher sites is provided in chapter 19. Also, it is important that any collection of textbooks be supported by a collection of professional education resources that provide information about textbook availability, reviews, and utilization practices. A list of these resources is provided in chapter 8.

Notes

1. *Collection Development Policy: Curriculum Resources Laboratory* (Iowa City: University of Iowa, 1993).

2. *Collection Development Policy: Curriculum Materials Center* (Moorhead, MN: Moorhead State University, n.d.), 26.

3. *Guidelines for Curriculum Materials Centers* (Cincinnati, OH: Academic Library Association Curriculum Materials Centers Interest Group, 1992), 2.

4. *Guidelines for Curriculum Materials Centers*, 2.

5. *Guidelines for Curriculum Materials Centers*, 8.

6. Association of College and Research Libraries, Education and Behavioral Sciences Section, *Curriculum Materials Center Collection Development Policy*, 2nd edition. (Chicago: American Library Association, 1993).

Chapter Four

K–12 Textbooks: Organizing the Collection

Textbooks can be either shelved as a separate collection or inter-shelved with other curriculum material formats such as curriculum guides and teaching activity books. Some CMCs prefer to shelve the various printed curriculum formats separately. Even though there can be some overlap in content among the formats, each basically serves a different purpose in the instructional process and corresponding access needs. See chapter 2 on curriculum guide organization for further discussion about usage patterns and shelving arrangements.

Classification/Call Number Considerations

No matter which way the textbooks are shelved, the classification system and the resulting call number configuration are very important elements for effective accessibility. A call number for a textbook should readily, without a lot of interpretation, identify the curriculum subject, publisher, grade level, date of publication, and edition type (teacher's edition, workbook, resource book, etc.). The format (textbook) should also be indicated. These components are necessary to satisfy the various needs for which the textbook format is selected. The order that these components take in the call number are based on the hierarchy with which the materials are accessed. If textbooks are shelved together separately from other curriculum materials, then the first component of the call number should be some indication that the material is a textbook. By shelving in the order that the components appear in the call number, all textbooks would be placed together. If textbooks are intershelved with other curriculum materials, the textbook indicator would probably occur at the end of the call number. Regardless of the format indicator, the order of the remaining call number components are as follows: first, an alpha or numeric indicator for the particular curriculum area; second, some indicator, cutter (the number that differentiates each volume), or otherwise, which represents textbooks by a particular publisher within that curriculum area; third, the publication date, so that editions by the same publisher are shelved chronologically (this is particularly important if multiple volumes exist for different years by the same publisher—the publication date is very useful in the call number so that a particular edition can be readily identified and the age of the textbook can be quickly seen); fourth, the grade level, so that materials in the same edition can be grouped together (this is more crucial for elementary grade materials than secondary level, but nevertheless, it is helpful to have it listed in the call number even if it is inclusive of multiple grades, e.g. 9–12, as it readily establishes the secondary level textbook); and finally, the grade level is followed by the edition type, i.e., teacher's edition, student edition, workbook, etc.

In preparation for this book, selected CMCs listed in the *Directory of Curriculum Materials Centers, 1990* were surveyed. The respondents represented colleges and universities in all areas of the country. Types of classification systems and call number construction were some of the data that were sought. Most CMCs use either Dewey Decimal or Library of Congress. Some, however, use the LT (textbook classification indicator of the Library of Congress), the Lois Watt's HEW classification system, or a homegrown system. The following examples will give an idea of the varied ways that CMCs handle the classification and call number construction of textbooks. Granted, some of the examples do not contain all of the recommended essential call number elements or recommended order mentioned above, but will give an idea of some of the varying patterns that may be followed. A listing of some of the various classification schemes appears at the end of the chapter.

Dewey Decimal Classification Scheme

Example 1

When using the Dewey Decimal System to classify curriculum materials, a decision must be made whether or not to use the 370s for elementary school materials, or just use all the regular class numbers for the various curriculum subjects, regardless of age level. CMCs have been found to do both. Below is an example of a Dewey classification scheme that does not use the 370s for classifying the subjects, but does use the Dewey class numbers as an indicator of the school level or audience for which the curriculum material was designed. This number is listed first in the call number so that materials in a certain grade range—e.g., elementary, secondary, early childhood—can be grouped together first. Many CMCs, however, no longer group their materials by age range on the shelf. The following scheme is one that places the textbooks on the shelf first by age range (first line of call number), followed by subject/format (second line), and then by publisher (third line). The fourth line of the call number indicates the grade level and edition type. No publication date is indicated. Below are the various designations used in the different lines of the call number:

School level

All	370.7	Elementary	372.24
Special	371.9	Secondary	373.07
Early	372.21		
Adult	374.07		

Subject

Regular Dewey classification numbers

Format

3: curriculum guide
4: teaching device
5: textbook

Edition type

These can be combined with one another, e.g., wt (teacher's edition of a workbook)

g: teacher's guide
k: key
L: laboratory manual
s: supplementary material
t: teacher's edition
w: workbook

Call number examples from this classification scheme

School Level:	372.24	elementary
Subject and Format:	5105	mathematics (510), textbook (5)
Publisher cutter:	H351h	Heath (*Heath Mathematics*)
Grade (if elementary) and edition type:	6t	sixth grade, teacher's edition
School Level:	373.07	secondary
Subject and Format:	5745	biology (574), textbook (5)
Publisher cutter:	P918p	Prentice-Hall
Grade (if elementary) and edition type:	L	laboratory manual

The CMC using the above scheme intershelves textbooks with curriculum guides and therefore does not indicate the format in the call number until after the subject class.

Example 2

The next classification/call number scheme uses Dewey also, but shelves its textbooks separately and therefore indicates the format (textbook) at the beginning of the call number. This is followed on the second line of the call number by the regular Dewey class number for the curriculum area. The third line provides the established abbreviation for the publisher. The edition date appears on the fourth line with the grade level following on the fifth line. (At times, some books have not only a grade level, but also a level indication within that grade. An example of the way this is handled in this system is given below.) The edition type is designated on the sixth line of the call number.

Below are edition type examples used in this system:

Edition type

TB—textbook (student edition)
TE—teacher's edition
WK—workbook
WKTE—workbook, teacher's edition
RB—resource book
DM—ditto master

Call number examples from this classification scheme

Format:	TEXT	textbook
Dewey subject:	574	biology
Publisher abbreviation:	HRW	Holt, Rinehart and Winston
Publication date:	1993	
Grade(s):	Gr 9–12	grades nine through twelve
Edition type:	TE	teacher's edition

Format:	TEXT	textbook
Dewey subject:	513	mathematics
Publisher abbreviation:	AD	Addison-Wesley
Publication date:	1995	
Grade(s):	Gr 2	grade two
Edition type:	TB	student's edition (textbook)

Format:	TEXT	textbook
Dewey subject:	428.4	reading
Publisher abbreviation:	HM	Houghton Mifflin
Publication date:	1993	
Grade(s):	Gr 2: Le1	grade 2, level 1
Edition type:	WKTE	teacher's edition of workbook

Library of Congress Classification Scheme

Example 1

If the Library of Congress (LC) is chosen to classify textbooks in the CMC, then a decision must be made, as in Dewey, whether or not the elementary level textbooks will be classified in LB range with the secondary materials classed in the regular subject letters. The alternative is to classify all materials, regardless of grade level, with the regular subject letters throughout. The following example uses the LC subject letters with no special assignment of elementary books to LB and is presented as an example of the modification that is possible. The CMC that uses this plan puts first emphasis on the subject, but rather than shelve all materials within that subject next by publisher, chooses instead to group the materials by grade level. The grade is spelled out, however, in the last line for clarity. No edition type is indicated.

Call number example from this classification scheme

LC subject and grade:	PE1119.1	reading (PE1119), 1st grade (.1)
Publisher cutter:	S58	Scott Foresman
Publication year:	1990 EF	year and title code (*Effective English*)
Grade:	Gr. 1	first grade

Example 2

The following example uses LC but configures the call number so that the edition type precedes the grade level. This would mean that all volumes in a series, for example, would be shelved together first by edition type and then by grade level. Therefore, all teacher's editions, student books, workbooks, etc., would be together. Each edition type then would be put in order by grade level. This method does not follow the usual way in which these materials are asked for, however. Usually a CMC user desires textbook materials on a given grade level. It helps to have all edition types together on the shelf by grade for that series to make this access easy. Of course, if the CMC is only buying teacher's editions this is a moot issue.

Call number examples from this classification scheme

LC subject:	QE26.2	earth science
Publisher cutter:	.S55	Silver Burdett & Ginn
Publication year:	1990	
Edition type:	T.E.	teacher's edition
Grade:	Gr. 7–9	grades 7–9

LC subject:	QA107	mathematics
Publisher cutter:	.H45	Heath
Publication year:	1994	
Edition type:	Wkbk	workbook
Grade:	Gr. 3	grade 3

LC subject:	H86	social studies
Publisher cutter:	.H38	Harcourt Brace Jovanovich
Publication year:	1991	
Edition type:	T.E.	teacher's edition
Grade(s):	Gr. 4	grade 4

LT Classification Scheme

The LT classification scheme was developed by the Library of Congress to classify textbooks. It is particularly helpful if a CMC desires to shelve all textbooks concerned with a particular broad discipline together. For example, all social studies textbooks would be shelved in one area, all language arts textbooks would be grouped together, etc. In the Dewey classification structure these broad curriculum areas sometimes get separated. For example, the social studies subjects of political science, elementary general social studies series, sociology, and economics are classed in the 300s while geography and history are classed in the 900s. The LT scheme uses four-digit numbers to represent the broad curriculum areas such as mathematics, science, social studies, foreign language, etc. Within this broad four-digit number, the subdivisions of the broad curriculum area are assigned a number. Below is shown how one CMC uses the LT classification scheme and constructs its call numbers. The four-digit LT subject number appears on the first line of the call number. On the second line appears the publisher cutter number. This is followed on the third line of the call number with a cutter for the main entry. The fourth line contains the publication date with the fifth line indicating the grade level. The last line designates the edition type. The following are examples of edition types being used with this classification scheme:

Edition type

te: teacher's edition
ts: tests
tm: teacher's manual
tr: teacher's resource book
dup: duplicating masters
sg: study guide
lm: laboratory manual
rbk: record book
wbk: workbook
sup: supplementary material

Call number examples from this classification scheme

LT subject:	4405	elementary math, K–8
Publisher cutter:	A33	Addison-Wesley
Main entry cutter:	A35m	*Addison-Wesley Mathematics*
Publication date:	1995	

Grade (volume):	4	grade 4
Edition type:	Wbk	student workbook

LT subject:	5220	chemistry
Publisher cutter:	M47	Merrill
Main entry cutter:	C42t	*Chemistry for Today*
Publication date:	1992	
Grade (volume):	10–12	grades 10–12
Edition type:	lm	laboratory manual

Lois Watt's HEW Textbook Classification Scheme

The Watt's classification scheme was developed by Lois Watts of the former U.S. Department of Health, Education, and Welfare, Office of Education. This scheme is similar to LC in that it initially divides the broad curriculum areas into a series of alphabetical letters. It is also similar to the LT system in that all subjects within a broad curriculum area such as language arts or social studies are classed together and then subdivided. Within a curriculum area, a given subdivision is displayed by decimal numbers. For example, mathematics is represented by "K" and algebra by ".3". The resulting first line of a call number for an algebra book would be "K.3". Spelling would be "E.12" ("E" for English Language Arts and ".12" for spelling). A cutter number is used for the publisher on the second line of the call number. This is followed on the third line by grade level(s) and the edition type. The fourth line contains the publication date. The following is an example of edition types being used with this classification scheme:

Edition type

s:	student's edition
t:	teacher's edition
m:	manual
mt:	teacher's manual
w:	workbook
wt:	workbook, teacher's edition
supp:	supplement (ary)

Call number examples from this classification scheme

Watt's subject:	S.52	earth science
Publisher cutter:	P91	Prentice-Hall

Grade and edition type:	6–9: t	grades 6–9: teacher's edition
Publication date:	1991	
Watt's subject:	H.22	U.S. history
Publisher cutter:	H68	Houghton Mifflin
Grade and edition type:	11: s	grade 11: student's edition
Publication date:	1995	

Other Local Textbook Classification Schemes

Some CMCs have developed their own classification schemes. Usually these locally designed or adapted systems are used just for textbooks, and sometimes for curriculum guides and audiovisual media, but the CMC uses Dewey or LC for children's books. Two examples of these schemes are described below.

Example 1

This first example uses a two-letter code on the first line of the call number to represent each broad curriculum area. This two-letter code is followed by a number which represents a subject subdivision within the broad curriculum area. The second line of the call number contains a publisher abbreviation followed by a two-digit publication date. On the third line appears the grade level or appropriate audience. Below is a good example of cataloging procedures for this system that clearly spells out and covers the various ways that the grade or audience should be represented. It provides for just about any situation that one encounters in working with textbooks. It could easily be used with any classification system.

"The third line will note the intended user level and will indicate the appropriate grade(s). If materials are of a general nature, an 'E', 'J' or 'S' shall be used to designate material for the elementary, junior or senior high school student respectively. No middle school designation will be used. 'E', 'J' and 'S' may be used together (i.e. 'E–J' or 'J–S'). When the specific grade is given on the intended curriculum materials it will be used alone. The following abbreviations will be used:

Abbreviation	*Designation*
K	Kindergarten
PP	Preprimer

PP1	Preprimer 1
PP1–3	Preprimer 1–3
P	Primer
1	First
2	Second
etc.	

The 'grade' will be the primary notation on the third line. When 'level' is provided it will follow immediately after the grade indicator enclosed in brackets. Example: 3(6) or grade 3, level 6. Items using a grade indicator and a first and second half breakdown will be noted with the grade followed immediately by a forward slash and then a 1 or 2 as appropriate. Example: 3/ 1 or 3/2.

For multiple grades, a '-' will be used; i.e., 1–6. Where material is designated for two grades or levels, the indicator will be separated by a comma (,); i.e., 1,1 +.

The letter 'P' will note post-secondary materials and the letter 'T' will designate teacher materials not associated with a basic curriculum package. 'EC' will note early childhood."[1]

Below are the abbreviations for the edition types that could appear on the fourth line of the call number.

Edition type

AG:	answer guide
BM:	blackline master
PG:	parent guide
RM:	resource material
SAB:	student activity book (includes workbooks and works designated to be in the student's hands)
ST:	student text
T:	test
TAB:	teacher's activity book
TAE:	teacher's annotated edition
TE:	teacher's edition
TRB:	teacher's resource book
TWB:	teacher's workbook

Examples of call numbers from this classification scheme

Subject (alpha)/ sub-category (numeric):	SC-6	physics

Publisher/year of publication:	HEA/94	Heath/1994
Grade:	S	secondary
Edition type:	TAE	teacher's annotated edition
Subject (alpha)/ sub-category (numeric):	LA-7	spelling
Publisher/year of publication:	MM/95	MacMillan/1995
Grade:	3	grade 3
Edition type:	TWB	teacher's workbook
	c 2	copy two

Example 2

The second example of a locally designed or adapted system begins its call number with a code for the format, e.g., textbook (Tx). This is followed by an alpha designator for the main subject and a second alpha designator for the subcategory. The publisher is developed from the cutter chart using the first two digits. This cutter is followed by the workmark for the title of the text or the title of the series in multiple volume sets. The grade level appears on the third line. If level designations are needed within a given grade, a letter is used to represent the level in the call number, e.g., Gr.1a, Gr.1b, Gr.1c, etc. If no grade is indicated, v.1, v.2, etc. is used. In this scheme, if a textbook is not part of a series and is not designated for one grade level, no grade is indicated and the call number only has three lines. One of the edition types below appears on the fourth line of the call number. Note that no publication date appears in the call number.

Edition type

pt. 1: student text
pt. 2: teacher's edition of text
pt. 3: student workbook
pt. 4: teacher's edition of workbook
pt. 5: test
pt. 6: teacher's edition of test

Call number examples from this classification scheme

Format.subject.sub-cat.:	Tx.So.ha	textbook.social stds.am history

Publisher:	S42a	Scott Foresman, *American Dreams*
Grade:	Gr. 11	grade 11
Edition type:	pt. 1	student text
Format.subject.sub-cat.:	Tx.L.R	textbook.lang.arts.reading
Publisher:	S42s	Scott Foresman, *Scott Foresman. Reading*
Grade:	Gr. 1b	grade 1, second level
Edition type:	pt. 2	teacher's edition of text

Examples of Call Number Classification Schemes

Dewey Classification Scheme

Algebra	512
Art	707
Biology	574
Calculus	515
Career Education	331.7
Chemistry	540
Composition (Writing)	426.23
Computers	001.64
Drama	811
Dramatics/Acting	792
Earth Science	550
Economics	330
English	420
English Grammar	425
Foreign Languages, General	410
French	448
Geography, Ohio	917.71
Geography, Regional	914–919
Geography, World/General	910
Geometry	516
German	438
Grammar	425
Guidance	371.4
Handwriting	426.34
Health	613
History, Ohio	977.1
History, U.S.	973
History, World/General	909
Journalism	070

Language Arts, General	420
Latin	478
Library Skills	025.5
Literature, American	810
Literature, English	820
Literature, General	800
Mathematics, Elementary/ General	513
Music	780
Physical Education	613.7
Physical Science	530
Physics	530
Poetry	811
Political Science	320
Problem Solving	160
Psychology	150
Reading	428.4
Science, Elementary/General	500
Social Studies, Elementary/ General	300
Sociology	301
Spanish	468
Special Education	371.9
Speech	426.22
Spelling	426.32
Study Skills	371.3
Thinking Skills	160
Trigonometry	516.2
Writing (Composition)	426.23

A chart of this scheme can be enlarged and displayed in the textbook area to assist users in locating materials in a particular subject area.

LT Classification Scheme

Foreign Language	2800
French	2810
German	2820
Latin	2840
Spanish	2860
Health and Physical Education	3300
Health and Hygiene	3320

Language Arts	4000
Elementary K–8	4010
Secondary 9–12 (General)	4015
Composition and Creative Writing	4020
English as a Second Language	4030
Grammar and Vocabulary	4040
Handwriting	4045
Journalism	4050
Library, Dictionary Skills	4060
Speech	4080
Spelling	4090
Reading	4200
Basal Readers	4210
Enrichment Readers, Reading Games	4220
Remedial Reading	4250
Reading Skills, Reading Comprehension,	4260
Content Area Reading, Reading Readiness,	
Phonics, ITA	4270
Diagnosis, Testing	4280
Literature	4300
Anthologies	4310
Biography	4314
Drama	4320
Essays	4324
Literacy Criticism	4330
Poetry (reading and writing)	4340
Mythology, Legends	4360
Science Fiction	4370
Mathematics	4400
Elementary Mathematics K–8	4405
General Mathematics	4408
Algebra	4410
Advanced Algebra	4411
Trigonometry	4413
Geometry	4420
Advanced Mathematics	4430
Calculus	4440
Analytic Geometry	4442
Probability and Statistics	4450
Applied Math/Consumer Math	4460
Computer Mathematics	4470
Science	5000
General Science	
Elementary K–8	5010

Secondary	5030
Applied Science	5040
Life Sciences	5100
Biology	5110
Anatomy and Physiology	5120
Physical Sciences	5200
Astronomy	5210
Chemistry	5220
Earth Science, Geology	5230
Environmental Science	5240
Marine Science, Oceanography	5250
Physics	5260
Social Studies	6000
Elementary K–6	6010
Economic, Legal, Political Systems	6020
Economics	6025
Law	6027
Geography	6030
Political Science, Government	6040
Psychology	6050
Sociology	6060
United States History	6070
State History	6075
World History	6080
Vocational Education	7000
Agricultural Education	7100
Agricultural Cooperative Training	7105
Agricultural Engineering Technology	7110
Agricultural Production and Management	7120
Forestry	7130
Homestead and Gardening Skills	7140
Natural Resources, Environment	7150
Horticulture	7160
Business and Office Education	7200
Accounting	7210
Communications	7215
Data Processing	7220
Economics	7225
Law	7230
Management	7240
Mathematics	7245
Office/Secretarial	7250
Record Keeping	7260
Shorthand	7270
Typewriting/Word Processing	7280

Watt's Classification Scheme

E   English Language Arts
      .1   Language Analysis and Skills
             .11   Penmanship
             .12   Spelling
             .13   Grammar
             .14   Linguistics
             .15   Phonetics
      .2   Basal Readers
             .212   Remedial Readers
      .3   Composition and Creative Writing
      .4   Literature
             .411   American Literature
             .4111   Afro-American
             .4112   Asian-American
             .4113   Hispanic-American
             .412   English Literature
      .5   Speech and Drama
F   Foreign Languages and Literature
             .120   Latin
             .121   French
             .122   Spanish
             .131   German
             .141   Russian
G   Guidance Services
      .1   Career Education
      .2   Educational Guidance
      .3   Social Guidance
H   Social Studies
      .1   World Geography
             .11   United States
             .111   Single states
             .112   Cities or towns
             .121   Single countries (use with DDC [Dewey
                        Decimal Classification] country number)
             .13   Physical Geography
      .2   World History
             .211   Single countries (use with DDC country
                        number)
             .22   United States History
             .223   Minority Group History
             .224   Unified course (history, civics, geography,
                        etc.)

.3 Global Cultural Studies (history, civics, geography, etc.)
.4 Government and Political Science
.5 Sociology
.6 Anthropology
.7 Economics

I (currently unassigned)

J Science
.1 General Science
.2 Biology
.3 Chemistry
.4 Physics
.5 Physical Science
  .52 Earth Science

K Mathematics
.1 Arithmetic
.2 General Mathematics
.3 Algebra
.4 Geometry
.5 Trigonometry
.6 Integrated Mathematics
.7 Calculus
.8 Metric System

L (currently unassigned)

M Humanities
.1 Performing Arts
.2 Visual Arts

N (currently unassigned)

O (currently unassigned)

P Religion (schedules undeveloped)

Q (currently unassigned)

R Health, Physical Education, and Safety
.1 Health and Hygiene
.2 Physical Education
.3 Safety Education
.4 Sports

S (currently unassigned)

T Industrial Arts and Vocational Education
.1 General Shop
.2 Drafting and Mechanical Drawing
.3 Building Trade
.4 Transportation and Communications
.5 Graphic Arts
.6 Control of Resources

.7   Home Economics
.8   Business Education

Other Local Textbook Classification Schemes

FA   Fine Arts
      FA-1   Art-Basic
      FA-2   Crafts
      FA-3   Art Appreciation
      FA-4   Music—Vocal
      FA-5   Music—Instrumental
      FA-6   Music Appreciation
      FA-7   Photography
FL   Foreign Languages
      FL-1   French
      FL-2   German
      FL-3   Latin
      FL-4   Russian
      FL-5   Spanish
      FL-6   English as a Second Language
HE   Health, Safety, Physical Education
      HE-1   Health and Safety
      HE-2   Physical Education
      HE-3   Sex Education
      HE-4   Alcohol and Drugs
HO   Home Economics
      HO-1   General Homemaking
      HO-2   Clothing and Textiles
      HO-3   Foods and Nutrition
      HO-4   Personal Development and Interpersonal
              Relationships
      HO-5   Child Development
HU   Humanities
LA   Language Arts
      LA-1   Reading
      LA-2   Literature
      LA-3   English
      LA-4   Journalism
      LA-5   Handwriting and Penmanship
      LA-6   Speech and Communication
      LA-7   Spelling and Phonics
      LA-8   Theater and Drama/Puppets
LM   Library/Media

MA   Mathematics
  MA-1   Arithmetic and Mathematics—Basic
  MA-2   Business and Consumer Mathematics
  MA-3   Algebra
  MA-4   Geometry
  MA-5   Trigonometry
  MA-6   Calculus
SC   Science
  SC-1   General Science
  SC-2   Biology
  SC-3   Physiology
  SC-4   Physical Science
  SC-5   Chemistry
  SC-6   Physics
  SC-7   Earth and Space Science
  SC-8   Ecology and Environmental Education
  SC-9   Life Science
SS   Social Studies
  SS-1   Social Studies—Basic
  SS-2   Geography
  SS-3   American History
  SS-4   American Government
  SS-5   Contemporary Issues
  SS-6   Civics
  SS-7   Economics
  SS-8   World History
  SS-9   Sociology
  SS-10 Psychology
  SS-11 State History
  SS-12 Anthropology/Archaeology
  SS-13 Law Related Education
  SS-14 Political Science
  SS-15 Religious Education
  SS-16 Multicultural
VA   Vocational and Technical Education
VB   Business and Commercial
  VB-1   General Business
  VB-1   Office Practice
  VB-3   Bookkeeping and Accounting
  VB-4   Typing
  VB-5   Shorthand
  VB-6   Business English
  VB-7   Business Law
  VB-8   Filing

VB-9   Business Machines
VB-10   Business and Data Processing
VI   Industrial Arts

Notes

1. *Learning Resource Center Curriculum Organization Chart* (Laramie: Learning Resource Center, University of Wyoming, n.d.).

Chapter Five

Teaching Activities: Acquiring and Organizing the Collection

Heavy demands are put on the curriculum materials collection for access to teaching activities and lesson plans. In the school setting, the learning process takes place as the student is put in touch with the curriculum through the teaching activities that the teacher has incorporated in the lesson plan. Preservice and inservice teachers know that the activities used are very crucial to whether or not success in meeting curriculum objectives is achieved. Therefore, these teachers are always looking for interesting and motivating teaching activities to use in their lesson plans. An additional type of resource related to this category is the bulletin board book. These books give various ideas and patterns for producing the "teaching" bulletin board and are also in great demand.

The curriculum materials collection must provide numerous teaching activity idea books covering a wide variety of curriculum topics. These include topics covered under the broad curriculum areas of science, social studies, mathematics, language arts, music, and art, as well as such areas as self-esteem, study skills, cooperative learning, and critical thinking skills. The *Guidelines for Curriculum Materials Centers* developed by a special committee of the CMC interest group of the Academic Library Association of Ohio states the following:

Teaching Activities and Bulletin Board Books
   a. This collection shall represent all major curriculum areas.
   b. Materials shall be distributed among early childhood, elementary, secondary, and special education as dictated by education student enrollment.

　c. This collection shall be added to annually with particular
　attention to new curriculum emphases and patterns.[1]

The *Guidelines* further states that for the category of teaching
activities and bulletin board books there should be at least four
titles for each full-time equivalent student enrolled in teacher education.[2] The complete *Guidelines* can be found in the appendix.

Acquiring Teaching Activities and Lesson Plan Books

There are many teaching activity books being published today.
The problem is that many of the publishers do not appear in regular acquisition sources. For example, one can look in the Teachers' Professional Books sections of *El-Hi Textbooks In Print* and
find only some of the teaching activity books being published.
Also, some curriculum librarians depend on approval plans to
provide announcements of newly published books and/or actual
books. Some of the publishers of teaching activity books are on
approval vendors' lists, but many are not. If one depends only on
approval plans to keep the collection supplied, many excellent
books will be missed and the collection of activity books will not
keep pace with the needs. The curriculum librarian must con-
stantly be proactive in the selection process for this area of the
collection.
　In preparation for this book, a number of sources to locate publishers of teaching activity books were researched. Once publishers were identified, catalogs were procured and analyses were
made to determine the curriculum areas covered by each publisher. The lists in chapter 13 and chapter 14 include some of the
more obscure publishers as well as the more commonly known
ones. If the curriculum materials librarian obtains catalogs from
these publishers and continues to receive new catalogs, he or she
will be kept current on new activity books being published. Ref-
erencing these catalogs will be useful to fill in gaps in the current
teaching activity book collection as well as to acquire additional
new books for the collection.

Organizing the Teaching Activities Collection

There are basically two ways that this collection can be arranged
for access. The books can be put in filing cabinets and arranged
by curriculum area, or placed on shelves. Since this collection is

heavily browsed with preservice and inservice teachers thumbing through many books at a sitting looking for lesson ideas, many CMCs place these books on shelves for ready and visible access.

Shelf organization of teaching activity books can follow different patterns. One method is to interfile these books with the professional education books of the library—the curriculum and instruction books which are more theoretical and research oriented. The drawback of this arrangement is that it does not provide quick access to just those books dealing with practical teaching activities, described and ready to be implemented. This browsing process is inhibited if these books are intershelved with the curriculum and methodology books for the area of study.

Another method of organization is to interfile the teaching activity books with curriculum guides and perhaps textbooks. Although this arrangement makes more sense than intershelving with professional education books because all books that can be used in lesson planning are together by subject, it still has its drawbacks. Many curriculum guides do not have teaching activities included, particularly of the longer, more descriptive type. Also, while teacher's editions of textbooks do have activity suggestions, individuals seeking ideas must go through a great amount of student material incorporated in the teacher's edition. While this may not necessarily be an undesirable or unfruitful activity, it can be inconvenient at times.

In working with preservice and inservice teachers and noting the usage patterns of the various curriculum materials, as well as meeting requests for quick access to practical teaching ideas, many CMCs find separating the teaching activity books collection from the other curriculum materials formats provides the best organizational pattern. If the students or teachers are beginning the process of designing a particular lesson plan, and need to find concepts, skills, or objectives for a particular grade level and curriculum area, they are referred to the curriculum guide collection where all of this material is conveniently shelved together. As the lesson planning process progresses and teaching activity ideas are needed, the next stop is the teaching activity collection where these books are shelved together by curriculum area and can be easily browsed for ideas. When teaching materials and resources are desired in the lesson plan, the individual can go to the textbook collection, audiovisual media and instructional materials collection, and perhaps the children's and young adult literature collection.

The discussion above has been emphasizing the practicality of arranging the teaching activity books as a separate collection on the shelves to meet the frequent browsing usage pattern. This does not mean to indicate, however, that this collection should not be in the catalog for access by author, subject, and title as well. Beyond browsing, there are those who need quick access to teaching activities on specific topics. Books in which major portions deal with particular curriculum areas such as learning centers, self-concept, critical thinking, environment, safety, literature-based, etc. should be accessible by subject heading. Many of the activity books will be found in cataloging utility databases such as OCLC, but some will have to be originally cataloged. The ideal, of course, would be for the curriculum materials librarian to be able to add subject headings from categories covered in a given book but not entered at the time of cataloging. An alternative would be to have input prior to cataloging. Time and policy, however, often make this impossible.

A classification system and call number structure must be found for the teaching activity books that works well with the curriculum materials collection as a whole with its various types of materials. Whatever classification scheme that is used is not so important with teaching activity books as long as there is some system that puts the books together by curriculum subject. Most of the books in this category will have teaching activities for various specific topics even if the book just deals with one broad curriculum area, such as social studies or science. Therefore, the class number used will be normally at a general subject level.

The call number structure is not as crucial as with curriculum guides and textbooks. Some indicator does need to be present telling the user that the particular title is a teaching activity book. The location of this indicator in the call number would depend on whether or not these types of books are intershelved with other types of books, such as textbooks and curriculum guides or professional education books. Usually, if intershelving is used, the teaching activity book indicator would be at the end of the call number. This would help the user find this category of desired book among the other types of materials. If teaching activity books are shelved together separately, as in many CMCs, the indicator would appear at the beginning of the call number as a prefix. However, crucial items needed in curriculum guide and textbook call numbers such as publisher information and publication date are not crucial for teaching activity books.

Each of these teaching activity books usually deals with activities for a particular curriculum subject area for a broad school level such as preschool, elementary, or secondary rather than each book dealing with activities for a particular grade level. Occasionally, a book will be more narrowly focused, such as primary or junior high level activities in a multiple curriculum, but not often enough to require a system which separates these on the shelf that discreetly. Usually either preschool, elementary, or secondary is enough as a grade level indicator. One of these appropriate broad school levels can be put in the call number of each book. An alternative is to group the preschool books, including kindergarten, separately on the shelf, especially since they usually deal with a variety of curriculum areas. The secondary level books could have a colored tape on their spines to indicate secondary level activity books. Those books without the tape would be elementary level activities.

A technique that is useful to users is color coding the curriculum areas. This is used in addition to shelf markers. This can be done in various ways. Since teaching activity books are usually paperback, they can be stored on the shelf in plastic pamphlet boxes, which provides stability. In addition, these boxes can be purchased from library supply companies in various colors. Particular colors can be identified for particular curriculum areas, for example, blue for social studies, red for language arts, green for science, etc. Another way to provide color differentiation is by sending the books to the bindery where they can be bound rather inexpensively in an economy binding with the covers mounted to the front. Various colors of binding can represent the different curriculum areas like the pamphlet boxes method described above. A color could be identified for those books that have a variety of curriculum areas in them and be given the category of "general." Of course, with the color coding system, some colors will be repeated, but at least teaching activities from the same curriculum areas are visually grouped together. This not only makes browsing easier, since one is usually looking for activities in a given curriculum area, but also provides stability for these normally paper-backed books for shelving, and endurance for circulation.

Bulletin board books can be shelved together as a category with an appropriate indicator in the call number. With a subject classification, all bulletin board books on a given subject will fall together for easy access. A color system could be used for these as well.

The teaching activity book collection is a most important part of any curriculum materials collection. Much thought and planning must go into just how to make this ever-growing collection readily available to the CMC clientele. By making it easily identifiable and the curriculum areas well defined, usage of this collection will soar.

Notes

1. *Guidelines for Curriculum Materials Centers* (Cincinnati, OH: Academic Library Association Curriculum Materials Centers Interest Group, 1992), 2.

2. *Guidelines for Curriculum Materials Centers*, 8.

Chapter Six

K–12 Audiovisual Media/ Instructional Materials: Acquiring and Organizing the Collection

It is imperative that the K–12 audiovisual media/instructional materials collection in a curriculum materials center be kept up to date. Also, there should be a variety of media types present in all of the curriculum areas, with good representation of the skills and concepts taught within each curriculum area and for the various grade levels. By maintaining a high quality collection, preservice and inservice teachers will have opportunities to develop their instructional materials selection, evaluation, and utilization skills as they prepare for and implement their lessons for on-campus class and clinical sessions, as well as field experiences.

The media and instructional materials collection is maintained in some teacher education curriculum materials centers merely as a sample or demonstration of what is available for teaching preschool through high school students. This type of collection does not adequately serve the goals of teacher education. If a teacher education student is practicing teaching methods through teaching a lesson or portion of a lesson in an on-campus setting, and only has at his or her disposal what can be produced, much can be lost in the experience. The same is true for those times when the student prepares and teaches a lesson in a field setting. If one must rely solely on what can be made or is available in the schools, again something less than appropriate can result. That is not to say that some schools do not have excellent instructional materials collections, but many do not. The teacher education student, however, is at the mercy of the school in which the field experience takes place. Furthermore, if the college CMC just has some "samples" of media, the student is really at a disadvantage in developing and improving his or her teaching skills. The *Guidelines for Curriculum Materials Centers* (see appendix) states that relative to media and instructional materials this collection "shall represent a range of curriculum concepts, skill, topics, and trends in preschool, elementary, and secondary school curriculums as well as exceptionalities, and professional education curriculum."[1]

While providing sufficient numbers of materials is an important issue, keeping the collection up-to-date is a key factor as well. Some CMCs have been funded well in the past and have a great number of materials, but because of recent funding cuts have not been keeping the collection current. As new technologies and materials are developed, the CMC should be on the cutting edge by having these materials available for students to see and become familiar with their use. Currentness is also imperative as more traditional materials, which may still be very valid as teaching materials, become out-of-date and need to be replaced. Funds must be provided so that appropriate weeding can take place and replacements be made to maintain adequate amounts of available materials. The CMC *Guidelines* states that this "collection shall be added to annually with particular attention to new curriculum emphases and patterns and technologies."[2]

In addition to adequate, current media and instructional materials, it is important that the CMC collection provide a *variety* of media types. Just a great collection of videocassettes, CD-ROMs, and charts does not adequately provide for the need of preservice and inservice teachers to become familiar with a wide range of media and instructional materials formats. They need to learn of the unique qualities of each format and how each contributes to the learning process in different ways and in different circumstances. The *Guidelines* states that this "collection shall contain a variety of formats, with both traditional resources and new technologies represented."[3]

Granted, funding levels drive the extent to which a local collection can be developed, but a certain minimum level needs to be established. The *Guidelines* recommends that there be a minimum of five media titles for each full-time equivalent teacher education student.[4]

An important aspect of developing the media and instructional materials collection is keeping up with where to purchase the media and instructional materials that are desired. These types of materials are rather elusive because they are not listed all together in a source such as *Books in Print*. If they were, the job of the curriculum materials librarian would be made much easier.

Usually one must use catalogs for accessing these materials, and this can become problematic because of time constraints to find materials on a certain topic or in a particular format. Also, it is difficult to even know of the many producers and distributors that are out there making available these materials and for which the librarian doesn't even have a catalog.

Not only does the curriculum librarian need to find materials to add to the CMC collection, but reference questions often come from clientele wishing to find instructional materials in a certain curriculum area or media format. The librarian should be able to direct these individuals to the appropriate producer or distributor. This makes it doubly important to know what the various sources of these materials are.

In preparation for this book, producers and distributors of media and instructional materials were researched in an effort to make it easier to access and obtain these kinds of materials. Some were familiar, but many others were not previously known. Catalogs from these sources were acquired and then analyzed as to the curriculum area and media format they make available. The research resulted in the lists in chapters 15 and 16. The first list could be used in cases where you are trying to increase your collection in a particular media or instructional material type. In this case you would be looking for producers and distributors of, for example, videodiscs, pictures, models, puppets, or manipulatives, etc. The producer or distributor appearing under each format is abbreviated; the abbreviations and the addresses for the companies they represent appear after the second list. The second list is arranged alphabetically by curriculum area with the various formats available listed under each area. The company abbreviations appear after the formats. This second list would be useful when the librarian wants to develop or update collection materials in a particular curriculum area, or patrons are inquiring where they might find media materials in a given area (e.g., study skills, mathematics, critical thinking skills, or children's literature, etc.). It is recommended that catalogs from the various producers and distributors be obtained to have on hand to use in conjunction with these lists for future acquisition purposes. The catalogs also make a nice reference collection to use with patrons along with the lists to answer media and instructional materials source questions.

Organizing the Collection

Curriculum materials centers primarily organize their audiovisual media/instructional materials in one of three ways or sometimes a combination of these. One pattern is to shelve/store the materials together by material type or format, i.e., all videocassettes are shelved together in one location, all overhead transparencies are shelved in another, and all games are placed with other games, etc. The advantage of this pattern, of course, is that shelving/storage units can be obtained that uniformly accommodate the usual size and shape of each material type making storage easier and more compact. The disadvantage is that the user is fragmented in trying to obtain various types of materials on the same curriculum topic and must go from one area to the next to find materials. Signage is very crucial in this arrangement so that the various material type areas are readily located.

Materials arranged by type need to have the format listed first in the call number to fix their location for the user. This media type code is then followed by an accession number, with all materials arranged in numerical order as received in the collection.

Example 1

Media type:	Videocassette (or, VC)

Accession number:	1
Media type:	Videocassette (or, VC)
Accession number:	2

Sometimes a broad abbreviation or class number is used to group materials of the same material type together by broad subject area. This is followed by an accession number representing the order it was received in the collection.

Example 2

Media type:	VC	Videocassette
Subject abbreviation:	SS	Social Studies
Accession number:	1	First received
Media type:	VC	Videocassette
Class number:	300	Social Studies
Accession number:	1	First received

Typically, the fuller cataloging/classification also has an additional line to represent a particular title. This is usually the first three letters of the title; some CMCs, however, use a publisher code instead.

Example 3

Media type:	VC	Videocassette
Class number:	973	History, U.S.
Title/code letters:	Ame	First 3 letters of title

For additional titles with identical media types and letters, an accession number can be added after the three letters of the title or publisher code to provide a more distinct call number.

Example 4

Media type:	VC	Videocassette
Class number:	645.1	Subject for 645.1
Title/code letters, and accession number:	Nut2	First 3 letters of title, and accession number 2

A second storage pattern is to intershelve all material types together by subject classification number. Therefore, one might encounter on the shelf in the Dewey classification number area 973.7, a game, a videocassette, a picture set, a chart, and a kit all dealing with the subject of the U.S. Civil War. Materials arranged following this pattern would need to display in the call number the subject classification code first, with the material type displayed usually last. The first three letters of the title would be used to make it distinct; an accession number could be added after the letters, as described in Example 4, to make the call number unique.

Example 5

Class number:	973	Subject for 973
Title/code letters:	AME	First 3 letters of title
Media type:	Videocassette (or, VC)	

The advantage of this arrangement is that the user can browse in a particular curriculum area for a variety of materials to use in a lesson. The disadvantage is that the various sizes and shapes of the materials make integrated storage difficult and more space is taken up on the shelves. Deep shelves are really a necessity for this pattern. Deep divider shelves work very nicely because materials can be contained better with dividers placed in various locations as needed, to keep flat items upright and tight.

The third pattern used by a smaller number of centers is to intershelve the media/instructional materials with trade books. In this case, not only would the various types of materials possibly exist together on the same shelf for a given classification, but books on the same subject would also be shelved there. The advantage, of course, is that print and nonprint materials are all together, which provides "one stop shopping" for the user. Also, this will hopefully stimulate teachers to use a multisensory approach in their teaching as well. The obvious disadvantage is the shelving of many different shapes and sizes along with books of different sizes. Again, as mentioned above, deep divider shelves are probably the best storage option for this pattern. Dividers would be used liberally to keep the books contained among the media. The disadvantage, however, is that by using deep shelves to accommodate the various media/instructional materials, the books, even though they are generally contained between dividers, tend to get pushed back in the shelves and are not, therefore, readily seen.

Some curriculum materials centers use a combination of the first two patterns. Some materials, such as kits, games, picture sets, models, etc. are intershelved, while other materials, such as CD-ROMs, audiocassettes, videodiscs, bulletin board sets, charts, etc. are shelved separately by material type. Some of the above materials are shelved separately for security reasons while the others are shelved separately because of size or other physical characteristic. Usually, though, the call number construction is consistent, with the media type always appearing in the same location in the call number. (See chapter 4 for the various classification codes which can be utilized for organizing materials.)

When particular items need to be kept secure by keeping the items shelved behind a service desk, a problem immediately occurs in that the CMC clientele cannot browse these collections, especially in a specific subject classification number or classification range. This browsing is especially helpful for reading descriptions that are usually on the material. A product called a browser pack is available from some library supply companies that will help solve this problem of maintaining security, while at the same time making material descriptions available. A browser pack consists of a plastic windowed sleeve in which may be put a copy of the description that is on the material container along with the title, call number, perhaps the grade level, and any other information that you want to include. A special bin can be procured in which to put these browser packs. The bin can then be put out in the open materials area in the CMC so that clientele can readily browse. Once an item is selected from the browser bin, it can then be procured at the desk.

No matter how this collection is organized for access, it is imperative that specialized containers be provided for the various types of materials. Items not only need to be appropriately preserved during circulations, but the user will also want to find the materials as a complete set. For example, some videocassettes come with comprehensive teaching guides that are 8.5 × 11 inches in size. These large guides could be rubber banded to the videocassette and placed on the shelf, but as so often happens the rubber band soon breaks or somehow the guide becomes separated from the video. A better solution is to buy some of the larger videocassette cases to have available for this situation. The large guide and videocassette all fit into the case and are very nicely kept together. The contents can be put on the outside of the case to verify that during circulation all parts go out and that all parts are returned. Also available are multiple video cases, cases for CD-ROMs with literature pockets, cases for videodiscs, book/audiocassettes, computer software, and audiocassettes. Puppets are neatly organized and accessed by placing them in see-through bags. Small puppets display well in the Monaco plastic hanging bags and can be hung on a rack for ready access and visibility. Large puppets can be stored in mesh bags with draw strings. In addition, special media boxes often need to be purchased for storing various kit materials. The above containers are often necessary because some producers do not adequately package their materials for a CMC environment. Sometimes the projected use for the material is in a classroom where the material resides all of the time or at least stays in one school building. When the material receives many circulations and must go from a college campus to local schools and vice versa, extra steps must be taken to adequately preserve the items by means of placing them in appropriate containers. Even though this packaging or repackaging requires extra funding, it is money well invested.

Notes

1. *Guidelines for Curriculum Materials Centers* (Cincinnati, OH: Academic Library Association Curriculum Materials Centers Interest Group, 1992), 1–2.

2. *Guidelines for Curriculum Materials Centers*, 2.

3. *Guidelines for Curriculum Materials Centers*, 1.

4. *Guidelines for Curriculum Materials Centers*, 8.

Chapter Seven

Access to Curriculum Materials and Sources on the Internet

Until now, this book has focused on acquiring curriculum materials that will be physically added to the CMC collection. In addition to making a variety of materials available inhouse for users, there is a need for the CMC to provide access to curriculum materials beyond its walls. The Internet has a vast amount of resources related to the preschool through high school curriculum and its instruction, and it is one way to provide this extended access. Online access can be made to curriculum guides, frameworks, and standards as well as many teaching activities. Also, the Internet has a vast amount of support material that can provide teachers and students with curriculum content having descriptive material, including pictorial, graphic, and audio representations. These can be invaluable in teaching a concept or skill. Chapters 18 through 22 list some of the curriculum materials sites on the World Wide Web. This is only meant to be a start, as sites and links appear and disappear on a regular basis. Those sites that indicate when they have been updated are especially useful for verifying currency. This list can be useful as the curriculum materials librarian works with users to find resources, as well as for instruction sessions with curriculum and methods classes and as possible links for a home page developed by the CMC. Chapter 18 provides curriculum guide, frameworks, and standards sites; chapter 19 lists textbook publisher sites; chapter 20, teaching activity sources; chapter 21, teaching activity sources by subject; and chapter 22 has curriculum content resource sites.

Chapter Eight

Professional Education Resources to Support the Curriculum Materials Collection

Recommended Professional Resources/Reference Books to Support the Curriculum Guide Collection

In addition to being excellent selection tools, the following three books provide great resources to your users looking for sources of curriculum guides:

Association for Supervision and Curriculum Development. Curriculum/Technology Resource Center. *The . . . Curriculum Materials Directory* (Alexandria, VA: Association for Supervision and Curriculum Development, annual).

Commended English Language Arts Curriculum Guides, K–12 (Urbana, IL: National Council of Teachers of English, 1994).

Exemplary Art Curricula: A Guide to Guides (Reston, VA: National Art Education Association, 1994).

The following is a subject list of selected publications that are published by professional associations or grant projects and are recommended for a CMC curriculum guide collection, or at least as support material for that collection. Most of these books provide curriculum standards and guidelines for the various disciplines and levels taught in the schools.

Art

Smith, Ralph. *Excellence II: The Continuing Quest in Art Education.* (Reston, VA: National Art Education Association, 1995).

Early Childhood

Dodge, Diane Trister, and Laura J. Colker. *The Creative Curriculum for Early Childhood* (Washington, DC: Teaching Strategies, 1992).

General

Bodell, Heather. *Goals 2000, A National Framework for America's Schools* (Arlington, VA: Education Funding Research Council, 1994).

Kendall, John S., and Robert J. Marzano. *Content Knowledge: A Compendium of Standards and Benchmarks for K–12 Education* (Longmont, CO: SOPRIS WEST, 1996). (Also available on CD-ROM and on software for Macintosh and Windows.)

Language Arts

National Council of Teachers of English. *Standards for the English Language Arts* (Urbana, IL: National Council of Teachers of English; Newark, DE: International Reading Association, 1996).

Mathematics

A Core Curriculum—Making Mathematics Count for Everyone: Addenda Series, Grades 9–12 (Reston, VA: National Council of Teachers of Mathematics, 1992).

Curriculum and Evaluation Standards for School Mathematics (Reston, VA: National Council of Teachers of Mathematics, 1989).

Mathematics and Science Standards: A Policymaker's Primer (Denver, CO: Education Commission of the States, 1994).

Science

Benchmarks for Science Literacy (New York: Oxford University Press, 1993).

Mathematics and Science Standards: A Policymaker's Primer (Denver, CO: Education Commission of the States, 1994).

National Science Education Standards (Washington, DC: National Academy Press, 1996).

Science for All Americans: A Project 2061 Report on Literacy Goals in Science, Mathematics, and Technology (Washington, DC: American Association for the Advancement of Science, 1989).

Social Studies

Expectations of Excellence: Curriculum Standards for Social Studies (Washington, DC: National Council for the Social Studies, 1994).

Geography for Life: National Geography Standards (Washington, DC: National Geographic Research & Exploration, 1994).

Implementing the American History Curriculum in Public Junior High Schools (Los Angeles: National Center for History in the Schools, University of California, 1994).

Lessons from History: Essential Understandings and Historical Perspectives Students Should Acquire (Los Angeles: National Center for History in the Schools, University of California, 1994).

National Standards for Civics and Government (Calabasas, CA: Center for Civic Education, 1994).

National Standards for History (Los Angeles: National Center for History in the Schools, University of California, 1996). (Revises and combines the below three history standards into one volume.)

National Standards for History for Grades K–4: Expanding Children's World in Time and Space (Los Angeles: National Center for History in the Schools, University of California, 1994).

National Standards for United States History: Exploring the American Experience (Grades 5–12) (Los Angeles: National Center for History in the Schools, University of California, 1994).

National Standards for World History: Exploring Paths to the Present (Grades 5–12) (Los Angeles: National Center for History in the Schools, University of California, 1994).

O'Shea, David. *Implementing the American History Curriculum in Public Middle Schools* (Los Angeles: National Center for History in the Schools, University of California, 1994).

―――. *Implementing the American History Curriculum in Public Senior High Schools* (Los Angeles: National Center for History in the Schools, University of California, 1994).

―――. *Implementing the World History Curriculum in Public Senior High Schools* (Los Angeles: National Center for History in the Schools, University of California, 1994).

Social Studies Curriculum Planning Resources (Washington, DC: National Council for the Social Studies, 1990).

The following books contain model curriculum guides and list available state-level curriculum frameworks for the subject with which each book is concerned. These books are available from

Corwin Press; 2455 Teller Road; Thousand Oaks, CA 91320-2218; 805-499-9734.

English as a Second Language Curriculum Resource Handbook: A Practical Guide for K–12 ESL Programs (Thousand Oaks, CA: Corwin Press, 1993).

English/Language Arts Curriculum Resource Handbook: A Practical Guide for K–12 English/Language Arts Curriculum (Thousand Oaks, CA: Corwin Press, 1992).

Mathematics Teacher Resource Handbook: A Practical Guide for K–12 Curriculum (Thousand Oaks, CA: Corwin Press, 1993).

Science Curriculum Resource Handbook: A Practical Guide for K–12 Science Curriculum (Thousand Oaks, CA: Corwin Press, 1992).

Social Studies Curriculum Resource Handbook: A Practical Guide for K–12 Social Studies Curriculum (Thousand Oaks, CA: Corwin Press, 1992).

Visual Arts Teacher Resource Handbook: A Practical Guide for Teaching K–12 Visual Arts (Thousand Oaks, CA: Corwin Press, 1993).

Chapter 23 contains a selected list of professional associations that provide curricular materials.

Recommended Professional Resources and Reference Books to Support the Textbook Collection

The following books contain the adopted textbooks for the subject with which each book is concerned for states that have statewide textbook adoption plans. See above for bibliographic information.

English as a Second Language Curriculum Resource Handbook: A Practical Guide for K–12 ESL Programs.

English/Language Arts Curriculum Resource Handbook: A Practical Guide for K–12 English/Language Arts Curriculum.

Mathematics Teacher Resource Handbook: A Practical Guide for K–12 Curriculum.

Science Curriculum Resource Handbook: A Practical Guide for K–12 Science Curriculum.

Social Studies Curriculum Resource Handbook: A Practical Guide for K–12 Social Studies Curriculum.

Visual Arts Teacher Resource Handbook: A Practical Guide for Teaching K–12 Visual Arts.

The following series of books, *Brown's Directories of Instructional Programs*, is distributed by the Association for Supervision and Curriculum Development. The books are updated annually and describe the various textbook programs and components published, including scope and sequence, skills covered, assessment formats, and connections to other resources.

Brown Publishing Network, *Brown's Directory of Instructional Programs (7–12): Foreign Language* (Mendham, NJ: Infinity Impressions, annual).

————. *Brown's Directory of Instructional Programs (7–12): Home Economics, Vocational Education, Technology Education, Arts Education* (Mendham, NJ: Infinity Impressions, annual).

————. *Brown's Directory of Instructional Programs (7–12): Language Arts* (Mendham, NJ: Infinity Impressions, annual).

————. *Brown's Directory of Instructional Programs (7–12): Mathematics* (Mendham, NJ: Infinity Impressions, annual).

————. *Brown's Directory of Instructional Programs (7–12): Science/Health* (Mendham, NJ: Infinity Impressions, annual).

————. *Brown's Directory of Instructional Programs (7–12): Social Studies* (Mendham, NJ: Infinity Impressions, annual).

————. *Brown's Directory of Instructional Programs (K–8): Language Arts/Reading* (Mendham, NJ: Infinity Impressions, annual).

————. *Brown's Directory of Instructional Programs (K–8): Language Arts/Spelling/Handwriting* (Mendham, NJ: Infinity Impressions, annual).

————. *Brown's Directory of Instructional Programs (K–8): Mathematics* (Mendham, NJ: Infinity Impressions, annual).

————. *Brown's Directory of Instructional Programs (K–8): Science/Health* (Mendham, NJ: Infinity Impressions, annual).

————. *Brown's Directory of Instructional Programs (K–8): Social Studies* (Mendham, NJ: Infinity Impressions, annual).

————. *Brown's Directory of Instructional Programs (K–8): Whole Language/Literature* (Mendham, NJ: Infinity Impressions, annual).

Other resource and reference books that support the textbook collection:

Ball, Deborah. *Using Textbooks and Teachers' Guides: What Beginning Elementary Teachers Learn and What They Need to Know* (East Lansing, MI: Institute for Research on Teaching, Michigan State University, 1986). (Contains textbook evaluation guidelines.)

Britton, Bruce K., ed. *Learning from Textbooks: Theory and Practice* (Hillsdale, NJ: L. Erlbaum Associates, 1993).

Cody, Caroline B. *A Policymaker's Guide to Textbook Selection* (Alexandria, VA: National Association of State Boards of Education, 1986).

Curriculum Review (Chicago, IL: Curriculum Advisory Service). (This is a journal published five times a year; some newly published textbooks are reviewed.)

El-Hi Textbooks and Serials in Print (New York: Bowker, annual). (Provides a listing of K–12 textbooks currently in print with access by subject, author, title, and series.)

Guidelines for Judging and Selecting Elementary Language Arts Textbooks (Urbana, IL: National Council of Teachers of English, 1990). (Provides eight guidelines that reflect current theory and research on language learning and gives criteria for evaluating text materials.)

Instructional Materials: Selected Guidelines and Resources (Washington, DC: National Education Association, Professional and Organizational Development, Instruction and Professional Development, 1989).

Woodward, Arthur. *Textbooks in School and Society: An Annotated Bibliography and Guide to Research* (New York: Garland, 1988).

Recommended Professional Resources and Reference Books to Support the Audiovisual Media/Instructional Materials Collection

The following resources are excellent for supporting the audiovisual media/instructional materials in the collection and for providing information about various available materials.

The African-American Experience: An HBJ Resource Guide for the Multicultural Classroom (Orlando, FL: Harcourt Brace Jovanovich, 1993).

Atkinson, Doug. *Videos for Kids: The Essential, Indispensable Parent's Guide to Children's Movies on Video* (Rocklin, CA: Prima Publishers, 1995).

AV Market Place (New York: R.R. Bowker, annual).

Bain, Amy J., Janet S. Richer, and Janet A. Weckman. *Solomon Resource Guide: Science,* 2 vols. (Cincinnati, OH: Solomon Publishing, 1994).

Bilingual Educational Publications in Print Including Audio-visual Materials (New York: R.R. Bowker, 1983).

Bittinger, Gayle, and Kathleen Cubley, eds. *One Thousand One Teaching Props: Simple Props to Make for Working with Young Children* (Everett, WA: Warren Publishing House, 1992).

Blenz-Clucas, Beth, and Gloria Gribble. *Recommended Videos for Schools* (Santa Barbara, CA: ABC-CLIO, 1991).

Bowker's Complete Video Directory (New York: R.R. Bowker, 1994, irregular).

Brophy, Jere E. *Distinctive Curriculum Materials in K–6 Social Studies* (East Lansing, MI: The Center for the Learning and Teaching of Elementary Subjects, Institute for Research on Teaching, Michigan State University, 1991).

Brown, David. *Goldmine: Resources for Teachers: Finding Free & Low-Cost Resources for Teaching* (Brookfield, VT: Ashgate Publishing Company, 1993).

Burroughs, Lea. *Introducing Children to the Arts: A Practical Guide for Librarians and Educators* (Boston: G.K. Hall, 1988).

Catalog of Captioned Educational Videos and Films (Washington, DC: Captioning and Adaptation Branch, Office of Special Education and Rehabilitative Services, U.S. Department of Education, 1994, annual).

Children's Media Market Place (Syracuse, NY: Neal-Schuman Publishers, irregular).

Clegg, Luther B., Etta Miller, and William H. Vanderhoff. *Celebrating Diversity: A Multicultural Resource* (New York: Delmar Publishers, 1995).

Diagram Group. *Charts on File* (New York: Facts on File, 1988).

———. *The Human Body on File* (New York: Facts on File, 1983).

———. *Junior Science on File* (New York: Facts on File, 1991).

———. *Time Lines on File* (New York: Facts on File, 1988).

Educational Media & Technology Yearbook (Littleton, CO: Libraries Unlimited, annual).

The . . . Educational Software Preview Guide (Redwood City, CA: Educational Software Evaluation Consortium, annual).

Guide to Free Computer Materials (Randolph, WI: Educators Progress Service, annual).

Educators Guide to Free Films, Filmstrips, and Slides (Randolph, WI: Educators Progress Service, annual).

Educators Guide to Free Health, Physical Education, and Recreation Materials (Randolph, WI: Educators Progress Service, annual).

Educators Guide to Free Science Materials (Randolph, WI: Educators Progress Service, annual).

Educators Guide to Free Teaching Aids (Randolph, WI: Educators Progress Service, annual).

Educators Guide to Free Videotapes (Randolph, WI: Educators Progress Service, annual).

EPIE Institute. *The Latest and Best of TESS: The Educational Software Selector* (Hampton Bays, New York: EPIE Institute, 1993).

Facts on File. State Maps on File (New York: Facts on File, 1984).

Find It! A Resource Guide to Hands-on Math (Pleasantville, NY: ScienceWorks, 1989).

Friedes, Harriet. *The Preschool Resource Guide: Educating and Entertaining Children Ages Two through Five* (New York: Plenum Press, 1993).

Gallant, Jennifer Jung. *Best Videos for Children and Young Adults: A Core Collection for Libraries* (Santa Barbara, CA: ABC-CLIO, 1990).

Geography on File (New York: Facts on File, 1991).

Giese, James R., and Laurel R. Singleton. *U.S. History: A Resource Book for Secondary Schools* (Santa Barbara, CA: ABC-CLIO, 1989).

Glade, Mary Elizabeth. *Review of Resources Teaching Law and the Constitution* (Boulder, CO: Social Science Education Consortium, 1987).

Goodman, Kenneth S., Lois Bridges Bird, and Yetta M. Goodman. *The Whole Language Catalog* (Santa Rosa, CA: American School Publishers, 1991).

Harrington, Barry, and Beth Christensen. *Unbelievably Good Deals That You Absolutely Can't Get Unless You're a Teacher* (New York: R.R. Bowker, 1995).

Hartog, Martin D. *Mathematics Education Resources: An Annotated Bibliography* (Columbus, OH: ERIC Clearinghouse for Science, Mathematics, and Environmental Education, 1994).

Hayden, Carla D. *Venture into Cultures: A Resource Book of Multicultural Materials* (Chicago: American Library Association, 1992).

High/Scope Buyer's Guide to Children's Software (Ypsilanti, MI: High/Scope Press, 1992).

Hill, A. David, and Regina McCormick. *Geography: A Resource Book for Secondary Schools* (Santa Barbara, CA: ABC-CLIO, 1989).

Hoffman, Audrea C., and Ann M. Glannon. *Kits, Games, and Manipulatives for the Elementary School Classroom: A Source Book* (New York: Garland, 1993).

Instructional Materials: Selected Guidelines and Resources (Washington, DC: National Education Association, Professional and Organizational Development, Instruction and Professional Development, 1989).

Junior Science Experiments on File (New York: Facts on File, 1994).

Lambert, David. *Earth Science on File* (New York: Facts on File, Inc., 1988).

Lobdell, James E. *Video Resources for the Teaching of Literacy: An Annotated Bibliography* (Berkeley, CA: Center for the Study of Writing, University of California; Pittsburgh, PA: Center for the Study of Writing, Carnegie Mellon University, 1993).

Martin Greenwald Associates. *Historical Maps on File* (New York: Facts on File, 1981).

Moss, Joyce. *From Page to Screen: Children's and Young Adult Books on Film and Video* (Detroit, MI: Gale Research, 1992).

Moyer, Joan, ed. *Selecting Educational Equipment & Materials for School & Home* (Wheaton, MD: Association for Childhood Education International, 1995).

The Multimedia and Videodisc Compendium for Education and Training (St. Paul, MN: Emerging Technology Consultants, annual).

National Information Center for Educational Media, *Audiocassette and Compact Disc Finder: A Subject Guide to Educational and Literary Materials on Audiocassettes and Compact Discs* (Medford, NJ: Plexus Publishing, 1993).

———. *Film & Video Finder*, 3 vols. (Medford, NJ: Plexus Publishing, 1997).

———. *Filmstrips and Slide Set Finder* (Medford, NJ: Plexus Publishing, 1990).

———. *Index to AV Producers and Distributors* (Medford, NJ: Plexus Publishing, 1997).

Neill, Shirley Boes, and George W. Neill. *Only the Best: Annual Guide to Highest-Rated Education Software/Multimedia Preschool–Grade 12* (Carmichael, CA: Education News Service, annual).

The Official Freebies for Teachers: Something for Nothing or Next to Nothing (Los Angeles: Lowell House, 1994).

Osborn, Susan. *Free (& Almost Free) Things for Teachers* (New York: Putnam, 1993).

Partin, Ronald L. *The Social Studies Teacher's Book of Lists* (Englewood Cliffs, NJ: Prentice Hall, 1992).

Pilger, Mary Anne. *Science Experiments Index for Young People* (Englewood, CO: Libraries Unlimited, 1988).

Science for Children: Resources for Teachers (Washington, DC: National Academy of Sciences, 1988).

Smallwood, Carol. *Free Resource Builder for Librarians and Teachers* (Jefferson, NC: McFarland, 1992).

———. *Health Resource Builder: Free and Inexpensive Materials for Librarians and Teachers* (Jefferson, NC: McFarland, 1988).

Sobel, Lester A. *Maps on File* (New York: Facts on File, 1981).

Software Reviews on File (New York: Facts on File, monthly).

Sorrow, Babara Head, and Betty S. Lumpkin. *CD-ROM for Librarians and Educators: A Resource Guide to Over 300 Instructional Programs* (Jefferson, NC: McFarland, 1993).

Summerfield, Ellen. *Crossing Cultures Through Film* (Yarmouth, ME: Intercultural Press, 1993).

Suttles, P. H. *Educators Guide to Free Social Studies Materials* (Randolph, WI: Educators Progress Service, annual).

Suttles, Patricia H., and Kathleen Suttles Nehmer. *Elementary Teachers' Guide to Free Curriculum Materials* (Randolph, WI: Educators Progress Service, annual).

Turner, Mary Jane, and Sara Lake. *U.S. Government: A Resource Book for Secondary Schools* (Santa Barbara, CA: ABC-CLIO, 1989).

The Video Source Book (Detroit, MI: Gale Research, 1997, annual).

Wayach, Robert B., and Richard C. Perney. *Approaches to World Studies: A Handbook for Curriculum Planners* (Boston: Allyn & Bacon, 1989).

Williams, Kim. *The Equipment Directory of Video, Computer, and Audio-visual Products* (Fairfax, VA: International Communications Industries Association, annual).

Words on Cassette (New York: R.R. Bowker, annual).

Words on Tape (Westport, CT: Meckler, 1984).

Part II

Resources

Chapter Nine

Curriculum Publications Sources

Below is a selected list of state departments of education and school systems that provide lists of available curriculum publications. If publication dates are routinely provided on their publications lists, this is so noted.

Alabama State Dept. of Education
Curriculum Development
Gordon Persons Building, Room 3339
50 North Ripley St.
Montgomery, AL 36130
(dates)

Alaska State Dept. of Education
Curriculum Office
801 West 10th St.
Juneau, AK 99801–1894

Arizona Dept. of Education
Curriculum Publications
1535 W. Jefferson
Phoenix, AZ 85007

California Dept. of Education
Bureau of Publications
P.O. Box 271
Sacramento, CA 95812–0271
(dates)

Delaware State Dept. of Education
Dept. of Public Instruction
Townsend Bldg.
P.O. Box 1402
Dover, DE 19903–1402

Georgia State Dept. of Education
Office of Instructional Programs
Division of Curriculum and Instruction
1952 Twin Towers East
Atlanta, GA 30334–5040
(dates)

Kentucky State Dept. of Education
Division of Publications Services
500 Mero St.
Frankfort, KY 40601

Louisiana Dept. of Education
Curriculum Publications
P.O. Box 94064
Baton Rouge, LA 70804–9064
(dates)

Minnesota State Dept. of Education
Department of Administration
Print Communications Division
Minnesota's Bookstore
117 University Ave.
St. Paul, MN 55155

Mississippi State Dept. of Education
Curriculum Publications
P.O. Box 771
Jackson, MS 39205–0771

Nebraska Dept. of Education
Curriculum Publications
P.O. Box 94987
Lincoln, NE 68509–4987
(dates)

New Jersey State Dept. of Education
Publications Office
CN500
Trenton, NJ 08625
(dates)

New York State Education Dept.
Bureau of Curriculum Development
Third Floor Education Bldg.
Albany, NY 12234
(dates)

North Dakota Dept. of Public Instruction
Curriculum Publications
600 East Boulevard Ave.
Bismarck, ND 58505–0440
(dates)

Ohio State Dept. of Education
Curriculum Publications
65 South Front St.
Columbus, OH 43266–0308

Commonwealth of Pennsylvania Dept. of Education
333 Market St.
Harrisburg, PA 17126–0333

South Carolina Dept. of Education
Curriculum Publications
Rutledge Bldg.
1429 Senate St.
Columbia, SC 29201

South Dakota Dept. of Education
Curriculum Publications
Richard F. Kneip Bldg.
Pierre, SD 57501

Texas Education Agency
Curriculum Publications
1701 North Congress Ave.
Austin, TX 78701–1494

Virginia Dept. of Education
Public Information and Publications
P.O. Box 2120
Richmond, VA 23216–2120

West Virginia State Dept. of Education
Public Information and Publications
1900 Washington St., East
Charleston, WV 25305

Wisconsin State Dept. of Public Instruction
Curriculum Publications
Drawer 179
Milwaukee, WI 53293–0179
(dates)

Clark County School District
Curriculum Office
601 North Ninth St.
Las Vegas, NV 89101

Dallas Independent School District
3700 Ross Avenue
P.O. Box 100
Dallas, TX 75204

Des Moines Independent Community School District
Office of Associate Superintendent for Teaching and Learning
1800 Grand Ave.
Des Moines, IA 50309–3382
(dates)

Fort Wayne Community Schools
Media Library
1511 Catalpa St.
Fort Wayne, IN 46802
(dates)

Fort Worth Public Schools
Curriculum Production and Distribution
100 North University Dr.
Suite 114
Fort Worth, TX 76107

Houston Independent School District
3830 Richmond Ave.
Houston, TX 77027–5838
(dates)

Jefferson County School District
Curriculum Publications
1829 Denver West Dr.
Building 27
Golden, CO 80401

Long Beach Unified School District
Office of Curriculum and Instructional Resources
Textbook Services
701 Locust Ave.
Long Beach, CA 90806
(dates)

Los Angeles Unified School District
Instructional Publications Unit
450 N. Grand Ave., Room G-390
Los Angeles, CA 90012

Milwaukee Public Schools
Division of Curriculum and Instruction
School Administration Bldg.
5225 W. Vliet St.
P.O. Box 2181
Milwaukee, WI 53201–2181
(dates)

Peoria Public Schools
Curriculum Office
3202 N. Wisconsin Ave.
Peoria, IL 61603
(dates)

Pittsburgh Public Schools
Division of Curriculum
Brashear Annex
590 Crane Ave.
Pittsburgh, PA 15216
(dates)

Portland Public Schools
Educational Media Dept.
501 N. Dixon St.
P.O. Box 3107
Portland, OR 97208
(dates)

Wichita Public Schools
Curriculum Services Division
201 N. Water
Wichita, KS 67202
(dates)

Chapter Ten

Textbook Publishers by Curriculum Area

This listing is by curriculum area and grade level. For each curriculum area/level, the publishers that specialize in textbooks for that subject and level are listed. Abbreviations used are defined in Chapter 12.

Art (Secondary)
G

Art (Elementary)
HB

Business (Secondary)
EMC G SW

Critical Thinking (Secondary)
EPS GF

Critical Thinking (Elementary)
EPS SV SP

English as a Second Language (Secondary)
AW BES G GF ML NDC NTC PH PHR

English as a Second Language (Elementary)

AW BES HB MCP NDC OC PHR SF TA

English as a Second Language (Preschool)

AW HB MCP SF

Foreign Language (Secondary)

Health: G
Language: DCH EMC G HRW ML NTC SF
Literature: BES
Mathematics: ML PH
Science: PH
Social Studies: BES GF SF

Foreign Language (Elementary)

Language: BES HM NTC SF SV
Literature: BES HB MMH MCP SP R
Mathematics: HB HM MMH
Reading: HM MMH WG R
Science: MMH MCP WG
Social Studies: HM MMH

Foreign Language (Preschool)

Language: HRW
Literature: BES SP
Mathematics: HB HRW MMH
Science: MMH WG
Social Studies: HRW MMH

Health (Secondary)

DCH G GF HRW PH SF SV

Health (Elementary)

HB MCP SF SV

High Interest/Low Readibility (Secondary)

Critical Thinking: GF
Health: GF

Literature: GF SP
Mathematics: GF
Reading: GF
Science: GF
Social Studies: BES GF
Study Skills: GF

High Interest/Low Readibility (Elementary)

Reading: CE MCP TA

Language Arts (Secondary)

DCH EPS G HRW ML PH

Language Arts (Elementary)

AW EPS HB HM MMH MCP SF SBG SRA SP

Language Arts (Preschool)

AW HM SRA

Literature (Secondary)

G HRW ML NE NTC PH SF

Literature (Elementary)

GL HB MCP OC SP TA WG R

Literature (Preschool)

HB SP TA WG R

Living Skills

GF

Mathematics (Secondary)

AW DSP DCH G HRW KCP ML PH SF

Mathematics (Elementary)

AW CTP DSP DCH EPS HB HM KCP MMH
NDE OC SF SBG SV R

Mathematics (Preschool)

AW DSP EPS HB HM MMH SF SBG R

Minority Studies (Secondary)

Literature: BES DCH GF HRW NE PH

Minority Studies (Elementary)

Language Arts: GL
Literature: BES MCP NE SP
Science: HB
Social Studies: MCP WG

Minority Studies (Preschool)

Literature: SP

Music (Secondary)

G

Music (Elementary)

HB MMH SBG

Music (Preschool)

MMH

Reading/Literacy (Elementary)

DCH EPS HB HM MMH MCP NDE OC SF SBG
SRA SV TA WG R

Reading/Literacy (Preschool)

EPS HB HM MMH MCP NDE SF SBG
SV TA WG R

Science (Secondary)

AW DSP DCH G HRW PH SF

Science (Elementary)

AW CTP DSP HB MMH MCP
SF SBG SV SP TA WG R

Science (Preschool)

AW DSP HB MMH SF SP TA WG R

Social Studies (Secondary)

AW G HRW ML NE PH SF SV

Social Studies (Elementary)

AW DCH GL HB HM MMH WG
MCP SF SBG SV SP

Social Studies (Preschool)

HB HM MMH SBG SP

Study Skills (Secondary)

EPS GF NTC

Study Skills (Elementary)

SV

Chapter Eleven

Ancillary Textbook Materials Publishers by Curriculum Area

The following is a list of ancillary materials, arranged by curriculum area, that publishers provide for use either with their textbooks or to be used as stand-alones. The term "supplementary" is used to denote those books published to be used either in addition to a basal book or in place of a basal book. Some of the textbook publishers include barcodes in guides or in the teacher's editions of the textbook for accessing the videodiscs that they market. This is noted in the videodisc categories below with the abbreviation (bc) after the publisher's abbreviation. Some publishers also provide software to allow interaction with videodiscs on a Level III basis. This is noted in the videodisc categories below with the abbreviation (i) after the publisher's abbreviation. If the publisher provides a foreign language version of the ancillary as well as English, this is noted by a (FL) appearing after the publisher abbreviation. The language is usually Spanish or an Asian language. Also, for the English as a Second Language materials, a subject area may appear after the publisher abbreviation to denote the curriculum area with which the material deals.

Art

Tradebooks	HB
Transparencies	G HB
Videocassettes	G

Business

| Audiocassettes | SW |
| CD-ROMs | G SW |

Computer Software	EMC G SW
Test Generator Software	SW
Transparencies	SW
Videocassettes	G SW
Videodiscs	G SW

Critical Thinking

Supplementary	EPS HM SV
Tradebooks	SP
Transparencies	SP

English as a Second Language

Audiocassettes	AW(reading) BES(social studies) G(mathematics) health, social studies) MMH ML(mathematics) NDC(language arts, social studies) NTC(language arts) PH(social studies) PHR(language arts) SF
Big Books	AW(reading) MMH
CD-ROMs	PHR(language arts)
Computer Software	ML(social studies) NDC(reading, mathematics)
Supplementary	AW(reading, language arts) NDC(reading, social studies) NTC(language arts) PHR(language arts) SF
Transparencies	MMH
Videocassettes	AW(language arts) PHR(language arts)
Videodiscs	G(health, social studies) ML(bc)(social studies, language arts, literature) PH(bc)(science)

Foreign Languages

Audiocassettes	DCH EMC G HRW HM MMH ML MCP NTC R SP SF S
Big Books	BES HM MMH MCP R SP WG
CD-ROMs	DCH EMC G HRW ML NTC
Compact Discs—Audio	EMC HRW ML
Computer Software	EMC ML

Supplementary	EMC HM MCP NTC SF
Test Generator Software	G HRW
Tradebooks	BES HB HM MCP R SP WG S
Transparencies	BES DCH EMC G HB HRW HM MMH MCP R SP WG S
Videocassettes	BES DCH EMC G ML
Videodiscs	DCH(bc) G HRW

Health

Audiocassettes	HRW SF
Big Books	MCP
CD-ROMs	G
Computer Software	G
Supplementary	GF MCP(FL) SF SV
Test Generator	G HRW PH
Transparencies	G HB HRW PH SF
Videocassettes	G HB PH
Videodiscs	G(bc)(i) PH(bc) SF(bc)

High Interest/Low Readability

Audiocassettes	MMH(reading, mathematics, science, social studies) ML(mathematics) MCP(literature) R(literature, reading) S(literature)
Big Books	BES(literature) MMH(reading, science, social studies) MCP(science) R(reading, literature) SP(literature) WG (reading, science)
Supplementary	MCP(health, science)
Tradebooks	HB(literature) MCP(literature) R(reading, literature) SP(literature, science) WG(reading, science) S(literature)
Transparencies	MMH(mathematics, reading, social studies)
Videocassettes	BES(literature)

Language Arts

Audiocassettes	G HB MMH SF SBG
Big Books	SRA
CD-ROMs	AW HB PH
Computer Software	DCH EPS G HB HRW PH
Supplementary	EPS GL HM SF
Test Generator Software	G
Tradebooks	SRA SP
Transparencies	DCH G HB HRW HM PH SBG SRA SP
Videocassettes	EPS G SBG
Videodiscs	G ML(bc) PH(bc)

Literature

Audiocassettes	G GF HB HRW MCP(FL) ML PH R(FL) SF SP WG TA S(FL)
Big Books	BES(FL) R(FL) SP(FL) TA S WG
CD-ROMs	HB SP
Manipulatives/Kits	ZB
Supplementary	GF GL NTC PH SF S
Test Generator Software	HRW
Tradebooks	BES(FL) HB(FL) MCP(FL) R(FL) SP(FL) TA S(FL) ZB WG
Transparencies	MCP R SF SP WG TA S ZB
Videocassettes	G HRW ML PH SP S
Videodiscs	ML(bc) PH(bc)

Living Skills

Supplementary	GF

Mathematics

Audiocassettes	G HM ML(FL) MMH(FL) R S
Big Books	CTP HB HM MMH MCP R SBG S
CD-ROMs	DCH PH SF SBG
Computer Software	AW DSP DCH G HB HRW HM KCP ML PH SF
Manipulatives/Kits	AW DCH HB HRW HM KCP MMH ML OC PH SF SBG
Supplementary	AW CTP DSP EPS GF HM KCP MCP NDE SF SBG SV

Test Generator Software	AW DCH G HRW ML PH
Tradebooks	DCH HB HM R S
Transparencies	DCH G HB HRW HM MMH(FL) ML PH R S
Videocassettes	ML SF SBG
Videodiscs	DCH(bc)(i) SF SBG

Minority Studies

Audiocassettes	MCP(literature)
Supplementary	GF GL(language arts) HB(social studies) MCP(social studies) NE PH(literature)
Tradebooks	BES(literature) MCP(literature) SP(literature) WG(social studies)
Videocassettes	SP
Videodiscs	HB(science)

Music

Big Books	SBG
Compact Discs—Audio	G MMH SBG
Computer Software	MMH SBG
Supplementary	MMH SBG
Tradebooks	HB
Transparencies	HB SBG
Videocassettes	G MMH SBG

Reading/Literacy

Audiocassettes	DCH HM MMH(FL) MCP NDE OC R SF SV WG(FL) TA S
Big Books	HB HM MMH(FL) MCP OC R(FL) SBG WG TA S
CD-ROMs	DCH HM MMH
Computer Software	HB OC SV
Supplementary	CE EPS MCP NDE OC SF SBG SV TA S
Tradebooks	DCH HB HM MMH MCP R(FL) WG(FL) TA S
Transparencies	DCH HB HM MMH(FL) MCP R WG TA S
Videocassettes	MMH
Videodiscs	HM(bc)

Science

Audiocassettes	AW HRW MMH(FL) R SBG S
Big Books	AW CTP MMH(FL) MCP(FL) R SF WG(FL) TA S
CD-ROMs	G HB HRW MMH PH SBG
Compact Discs—Audio	SBG
Computer Software	AW DCH G HB PH
Manipulatives/Kits	AW R SF SBG S
Supplementary	CTP DSP HM MCP(FL) SF SBG SV ZB
Test Generator Software	DCH G HRW PH
Tradebooks	AW HB R SP(FL) WG(FL) S
Transparencies	AW DCH G HB HRW MMH PH R SF SBG SP WG S
Videocassettes	AW DCH G HB MMH PH SF SBG S
Videodiscs	AW(bc) DCH(bc)(i) G(bc)(i) HB HRW(bc) MMH(bc)(i) PH (bc)(i) R(bc) SF(i) SBG

Social Studies

Audiocassettes	AW G GF HRW ML MMH(FL) PH SBG S
Big Books	MCP MMH(FL) SBG WG S
CD-ROMs	AW DCH G ML SF
Computer Software	AW DCH G HB HRW HM ML
Supplementary	AW EPS GF GL HRW HM ML MCP NE NTC SF SBG SV
Test Generator Software	AW G HRW ML PH SF S
Tradebooks	AW GF GL HRW HM ML MCP SF SBG SV WG
Transparencies	AW DCH G GF HB HM MMH(FL) ML PH SF SP WG S
Videocassettes	AW G HRW MMH ML PH SF SBG SP
Videodiscs	AW DCH(i) G(bc)(i) HRW(bc) MMH(bc) ML(bc) PH(bc)(i) SF(bc)(i)

Chapter Twelve

Textbook Publishers

This listing provides publishers' addresses, phone numbers, and abbreviations.

AW   Addison Wesley Publishing Co.
2725 Sand Hill Rd.
Menlo, CA 94025
415-854-0300

BES   Bilingual Educational Services, Inc.
2514 South Grand Avenue
Los Angeles, CA 90007-9979
800-448-6032

CE   Creative Education, Inc.
123 S. Broad St.
P.O. Box 227
Mankato, MN 56001
800-445-6209

CTP   Creative Teaching Press
Distributed by Abrams & Company Publishers, Inc.
61 Mattatuck Heights Road
Waterbury, CT 06705
800-227-9120

DSP   Dale Seymour Publications
P.O. Box 10888
Palo Alto, CA 94303
800-417-2321

DCH   D. C. Heath and Company
125 Spring Street
Lexington, MA 02173
800-334-3284

EPS   Educators Publishing Service, Inc.
           31 Smith Place
           Cambridge, MA 02138-1000
           800-225-5750

EMC   EMC Paradigm
           300 York Avenue
           St. Paul, MN 55101
           800-328-1452

G   Glencoe/McGraw-Hill
           P.O. Box 508
           Columbus, OH 43216
           800-334-7344

GF   Globe Fearon
           4350 Equity Drive
           P.O. Box 2649
           Columbus, OH 43216
           800-848-9500

GL   Graphic Learning
           61 Mattatuck Heights
           Waterbury, CT 06705
           800-874-0029

HB   Harcourt Brace and Company
           School Publishers
           6277 Sea Harbor Drive
           Orlando, FL 32887
           800-225-5425

HRW   Holt, Rinehart and Winston, Inc.
           6277 Sea Harbor Drive
           Orlando, FL 32821-9816
           800-225-5425
           (same as Harcourt Brace)

HM   Houghton Mifflin
           222 Berkeley Street
           Boston, MA 02116-3764
           800-733-2828

KCP   Key Curriculum Press
2512 Martin Luther King Jr. Way
P.O. Box 2304
Berkeley, CA 94702-0304
800-995-MATH

MMH   Macmillan/McGraw-Hill
220 East Danieldale Road
De Soto, TX 75115
800-442-9685

ML   McDougal Littell
P.O. Box 1667
Evanston, IL 60204
800-323-5435

MCP   Modern Curriculum Press
4350 Equity Drive
P.O. Box 2649
Columbus, OH 43216
800-321-3106

NDC   National Dissemination Center
50 Constitution Drive
Taunton, MA 02780
508-824-7188

NDE   New Dimensions in Education
61 Mattatuck Heights Road
Waterbury, CT 06705
800-227-9120

NE   Network of Educators on the Americas
P.O. Box 73038
Washington, DC 20056-3038
202-429-0137

NTC   NTC Publishing Group
4255 W. Touhy Avenue
Lincolnwood, IL 60646-1975
800-323-4900

OC   Open Court Publishing Company
315 Fifth Street
Peru, IL 61354-0599
800-435-6850

PH   Prentice Hall
            School Division of Simon & Schuster
            4350 Equity Drive
            P.O. Box 2649
            Columbus, OH 43272-4480
            800-848-9500

PHR   Prentice Hall Regents
            200 Old Tappan Road
            Old Tappan, NJ 07675
            800-223-1360

R   Rigby
            P.O. Box 797
            Crystal Lake, IL 60039-0797
            800-822-8661

S   Scholastic Inc.
            2931 E. McCarty Street
            Jefferson City, MO 65101
            800-3256149

SF   Scott Foresman
            1900 East Lake Avenue
            Glenview, IL 60025
            800-554-4411

SBG   Silver Burdett Ginn
            4350 Equity Drive
            P.O. Box 2649
            Columbus, OH 43216
            614-876-0371

SW   South-Western Educational Publishing
            5101 Madison Road
            Cincinnati, OH 45227
            800-354-9706

SRA   SRA
            P.O. Box 543
            Blacklick, OH 43004-9902
            800-843-8855

SV   Steck-Vaughn
P.O. Box 26015
Austin, TX 78755
800-531-5015

SP   Sundance Publishing
234 Taylor Street
P.O. Box 1326
Littleton, MA 01460-9936
800-343-8204

TA   Troll Associates
100 Corporate Drive
Mahwah, NJ 07430
800-929-TROLL

WG   The Wright Group
19201 120th Avenue NE
Bothell, WA 98011-9512
800-523-2371, ext. 303

ZB   Zaner-Bloser
2200 West Fifth Avenue
P.O. Box 16764
Columbus, OH 43216-6764
800-421-3018

Chapter Thirteen

Teaching Activities Sources by Curriculum Area

The following is a subject list of curriculum areas in which teaching activity books and lesson plans are published. Those publishers and sources that provide activity books for each area are included. Codes have been used to simplify the list. The complete list of publishers and sources with corresponding codes and addresses is provided in the next chapter, "Teaching Activities Publishers and Sources."

Art

CE, DS, D, EC, EM, GA, GB, GH, IP, JW, J, LBI, N, NAE, R, S, TCM, TIP, Z, HS, FS, T, TSD, A

Children's Literature-Based Lessons and Activities

CP

Children's Literature Units

ECS, EC, HPK, NU, P, SD, TCM, FS

Communication Disorders

ATP, CS, SRA

Cooperative Learning

CRP, ECS, EM, GA, IP, LPI, NR, S, TCM, WP, Z, T, TSD

Critical Thinking

AWP, AR, APC, BC, CE, CLP, CTP, DS, ECS, GA, GB, IP, JW, NR, SD, TCM, Z, HS, FS, DL

Foreign Language

E, EM, JW, NU, HS, TSD

Gifted

AWP, BC, CLP, GA, FSP, A, TIP

Guidance

GA, HE

Health

DP, HE, IN, NSP, HS

Interdisciplinary

AWP, AIM, CD, CS, CE, CRP, DE, D, ECS, E, EM, GA, HPK, JW, M, NR, NU, SSE, SRA, TCM, TIP, WP, Z, FS

Language Arts

AWP, BC, BL, CD, CS, CP, CW, CE, CT, CTP, DS, ECS, E, EM, GA, GB, GH, HPK, IP, IN, JW, LPI, LP, M, NAE, NCTE, NR, NU, O, P, R, S, TCM, TIP, TW, WP, Z, HS, FS, T, W, IF, TSD, FSP, DL, A

Learning Disabilities

BC

Literature-Based Lessons and Activities

AWP, BL, CD, CE, CRP, DE, ECS, EC, E, EM, FS, GA, HS, HPK, IP, IF, NU, O, P, S, SSE, SRA, SD, TCM, TIP, WP

Mathematics

AWP, AR, BC, CD, CE, CRP, CT, CTP, C, DS, DL, DE, D, E, ETA, EM, FS, GA, GB, HS, IP, IF, IN, JW, LP, MT, M, N, NAE, NCTM, NR, S, SRA, TCM, TIP, TL, T, WP, Z

Multicultural

BC, BL, BR, CD, CRP, DS, DL, ECS, EC, E, EM, FS, FSP, GA, GB, GH, JW, NCTM, P, S, SSE, SRA, SD, TSD, TCM, Z

Music

GA, HS, JW, NAE, R, TSD, Z

Preschool

A, CS, EC, E, EM, FS, GA, GB, GH, HS, IP, LPI, NAE, R, TSD, WP

Science

AWP, AR, AIM, APC, BC, CB, CD, CL, CE, CLP, CT, CTP, C, CV, DS, DL, DE, DP, D, ECS, E, ETA, EM, FS, GA, GB, GH, HS, IP, IF, IN, JW, LP, M, N, NAE, NR, NSTA, R, S, SK, SRA, SW, TCM, TIP, TL, T, WA, WP, Z

Science Fairs

AWP, CB, CLP, CV, ETA, GA, GB, M, N, SW, SK, WA

Self-Esteem

ATP, BC, FSP, GA, HE, JW, NR, Z

Social Studies

AWP, BC, BR, CD, CL, CE, CTP, DP, D, ECS, E, EM, FS, GA, GB, HS, IP, IF, IN, JW, M, NCSS, NR, S, SSE, SS, TSD, TIP, T, Z

Special Education

ATP, AP, BC, FSP, JW, LP, WP

Study Skills

GB, JW

Vocational

JW, LPI

Young Adult Literature-Based Lessons and Activities
CP

Young Adult Literature Units
BR, CL, ECS, HPK, JW, NU, P, SD, TPP, W

The following types of materials are useful to support teaching activities:

Bulletin Boards
A, CD, CE, EC, E, EM, GB, IP, N, TCM

Clip Art/Patterns
CD, CE, EC, E, IP, IF, TSD, TCM

Learning Centers
NU, S, SRA, TCM, EM, EC, ECS, CT, CE, AWP

Simulations
Social Studies—CE, IN, JW, S, SSE, SS
Science—S

Chapter Fourteen

Teaching Activities Publishers and Sources

AWP   A.W. Peller & Associates, Inc.
Educational Materials
210 Sixth Avenue
P.O. Box 106
Hawthorne, NJ 07507-0106
800-451-7450

ATP   Academic Therapy Publications
20 Commercial Blvd.
Novato, CA 94947-6191
415-883-3314

A   The Acorn
Bur Oak Press, Inc.
8717 Mockingbird Rd. S.
Platteville, WI 53818
608-348-8662

AR   Activity Resources Co., Inc.
P.O. Box 4875
Hayward, CA 94540
510-782-1300

AIM   AIMS Education Foundation
P.O. Box 8120
Fresno, CA 93747-8120
209-255-4094

AP   Alemany Press
Division of Janus Book Publishers, Inc.
2501 Industrial Pkwy, West
Dept. ESLRA
Hayward, CA 94545
800-227-2375

APC   Alpha Publishing Company, Inc.
           1910 Hidden Point Road
           Annapolis, MD 21401
           800-842-6696

BC   Beckley-Cardy
           1 East First Street
           Duluth, MN 55802
           800-446-1477

BL   Book Lures
           P.O. Box 0455
           O'Fallon, MO 63366-0455
           800-844-0455

BR   Brown-Roa
           P.O. Box 1028
           Dubuque, IA 52004-1028
           800-922-7696

CB   Carolina Biological Supply Company
           2700 York Road
           Burlington, NC 27215
           800-334-5551

CD   Carson-Dellosa Publishing Company, Inc.
           P.O. Box 35665
           Greensboro, NC 27425
           800-321-0943

CL   The Center for Learning
           P.O. Box 910
           Villa Maria, PA 16155
           800-767-9090

CS   Communication Skill Builders
           Division of The Psychological Corporation
           555 Academic Court
           San Antonio, TX 78204-2498
           800-228-0752

CV   Connecticut Valley Biological
           82 Valley Road
           P.O. Box 326
           Southampton, MA 01073
           413-527-4030

CP   Continental Press
            520 E. Bainbridge Street
            Elizabeth, PA 17022
            800-233-0759

CW   Cottonwood Press
            305 W. Magnolia, Suite 398
            Fort Collins, CO 80521
            800-864-4297

CE   Creative Educational Materials
            P.O. Box 18127
            West St. Paul, MN 55118-0127
            612-455-7511

CLP   Creative Learning Press, Inc.
            P.O. Box 320
            Mansfield Center, CT 06250
            203-429-8118

CRP   Creative Publications
            5623 W. 115th Street
            Worth, IL 60482-9931
            800-624-0822

CT   Creative Teaching Associates
            P.O. Box 7766
            Fresno, CA 93747-7766
            800-767-4282

CTP   Critical Thinking Press & Software
            P.O. Box 448
            Pacific Grove, CA 93950-0448
            800-458-4849

C   Cuisenaire Co. of America, Inc.
            P.O. Box 5026
            White Plains, NY 10602-5026
            800-237-3142

DS   Dale Seymour Publications
            P.O. Box 10888
            Palo Alto, CA 94303-0879
            800-827-1100

DL   Dandy Lion Publications
            3563 Sueldo, Suite L
            San Luis Obispo, CA 93401
            800-776-8032

DE   Delta Education
            P.O. Box 3000
            Nashua, NH 03061-3000
            800-442-5444

DP   Diane Publishing Co.
            600 Upland Ave.
            Upland, PA 19015-2442
            610-499-7415

D   Didax
            395 Main Street
            Rowley, MA 01969-3785
            800-458-0024

ECS   ECS Learning Systems, Inc.
            P.O. Box 791437
            San Antonio, TX 78279
            800-68-TEACH

EC   Education Center, Inc.
            1607 Battleground Avenue
            P.O. Box 9753
            Greensboro, NC 27429
            800-334-0298

E   Edumate Educational Materials
            2231 Morena Blvd.
            San Diego, CA 92110
            619-275-7117

ETA   ETA
            620 Lakeview Parkway
            Vernon Hills, IL 60061
            800-445-5985

EM   Evan-Moor Educational Publishers
            18 Lower Ragsdale Drive
            Monterey, CA 93940-5746
            800-777-4362

FS   Frank Schaffer Publications, Inc.
23740 Hawthorne Blvd.
P.O. Box 2853
Torrance, CA 90509-2853
800-421-5565

FSP   Free Spirit Publishing, Inc.
400 First Avenue North, Suite 616
Minneapolis, MN 55401-1730
800-735-7323

GA   Good Apple Fearon Teacher Aids
4350 Equity Drive
P.O. Box 2649
Columbus, OH 43216
800-321-3106

GB   Goodyear Books
1900 East Lake Avenue
Glenview, IL 60025
800-628-4480, ext. 3038

GH   Gryphon House, Inc.
P.O. Box 207
Beltsville, MD 20704-0207
800-638-0928

HS   Hayes School Publishing Co., Inc.
321 Pennwood Ave.
Pittsburgh, PA 15221-3398
800-245-6234

HE   Health Education Services
Division of Social Studies School Service
10200 Jefferson Boulevard, Room H31
Culver City, CA 90232-0802
800-421-4246

HPK   H.P. Kopplemann, Inc.
Paperbook Book Service
140 Van Block Ave
P.O. Box 145
Hartford, CT 06141-0145
800-842-2165

IP   Incentive Publications, Inc.
            3835 Cleghorn Avenue
            Nashville, TN 37215-2532
            800-421-2830

IF   Instructional Fair, Inc.
            P.O. Box 1650
            Grand Rapids, MI 49501
            800-253-5469

IN   Interact Company
            1825 Gillespie Way, #101
            El Cajon, CA 92020-1095
            800-359-0961

JW   J. Weston Walch, Publisher
            321 Valley Street
            P.O. Box 658
            Portland, ME 04104-0658
            800-341-6094

J   Judy/Instructo
            4350 Equity Drive
            P.O. Box 2649
            Columbus, OH 43216
            800-321-3106

LPI   Learning Publications, Inc.
            5351 Gulf Drive
            P.O. Box 1338
            Holmes Beach, FL 34218-1338
            800-222-1525

LP   Love Publishing Company
            1777 South Bellaire Street
            Denver, CO 80222
            303-757-2579

MT   Math Teachers Press, Inc.
            5100 Gamble Drive, Suite 398
            Minneapolis, MN 55416
            800-852-2435

M   Milliken Publishing Company
           1100 Research Blvd.
           P.O. Box 21579
           St. Louis, MO 63132
           800-325-4136

N   Nasco
           901 Janesville Ave.
           Fort Atkinson, WI 53538-0901
           414-563-2446
           800-558-9595
             OR
           4825 Stoddard Rd.
           Modesto, CA 95356-9318
           800-558-9595
           209-545-1600

NAE   National Association for the Education of Young
             Children
           1509 16th Street, N.W.
           Washington, DC 20036-1426
           800-424-2460

NCSS   National Council for the Social Studies
           3501 Newark Street, NW
           Washington, DC 20016

NCTE   National Council of Teachers of English
           1111 W. Kenyon Road
           Urbana, Illinois 61801-1096
           800-369-6283

NCTM   National Council of Teachers of Mathematics
           1906 Association Drive
           Reston, VA 22091-1593
           800-235-7566

NR   National Resource Center for Middle Grades
             Education
           University of South Florida
           College of Education—Room 118
           4202 Fowler Avenue
           Tampa, FL 33620-5650
           813-974-2530 (NSTA)

NSP   National School Products
           101 East Broadway
           Maryville, TN 37804-2498
           800-251-9124

NSTA   National Science Teachers Association
           NSTA Publication Sales
           1840 Wilson Boulevard
           Arlington, VA 22201-3000
           800-722-NSTA

NE   Network of Educators on the Americas
           P.O. Box 73038
           Washington, DC 20056-3038
           202-429-0137

NU   Novel Units
           P.O. Box 1461
           Palatine, IL 60078
           708-253-8200

O   Oryx Press
           4041 North Central Ave., Suite 700
           Phoenix, AZ 85012-3397
           800-279-6799

P   Perfection Learning
           1000 North Second Avenue
           Logan, IA 51546-1099
           800-831-4190

R   Redleaf Press
           450 North Syndicate, Suite 5
           St. Paul, MN 55104-4125
           800-423-8309

SW   Sargent-Welch
           911 Commerce Court
           Buffalo Grove, IL 60089-2375
           800-727-4368

S   Scholastic Professional Books
           P.O. Box 7502
           Jefferson City, MO 65101-9968
           800-325-6149

SK   Science Kit & Boreal Laboratories
            777 East Park Drive
            Tonawanda, NY 14150-6784
            800-828-7777

SSE   Social Science Education Consortium
            P.O. Box 21270
            Boulder, CO 80308-4270
            303-492-8154

SS   Social Studies School Service
            10200 Jefferson Boulevard
            Room B31
            P.O. Box 802
            Culver City, CA 90232-0802
            800-421-4246

SRA   SRA/McGraw-Hill
            P.O. Box 543
            Blacklick, OH 43004-0543
            800-843-8855

SD   Sundance Publishing
            234 Taylor Street
            P.O. Box 1326
            Littleton, MA 01460-9936
            800-343-8204

TSD   T.S. Dennison & Company, Inc.
            P.O. Box 1650
            Grand Rapids, MI 49501
            800-253-5469

TCM   Teacher Created Materials
            P.O. Box 1040
            Huntington Beach, CA 92647
            800-662-4321

TIP   Teacher Ideas Press
            Division of Libraries Unlimited
            Dept. K953
            P.O. Box 6633
            Englewood, CO 80155-6633
            800-237-6124

TPP   Teacher's Pet Publications, Inc.
            11504 Hammock Point
            Berlin, MD 21811
            800-255-8935

TW   Teachers & Writers Collaborative
            5 Union Square West
            New York, NY 10003-3306
            212-691-6590

TL   Teachers' Laboratory
            P.O. Box 6480
            Brattleboro, VT 05302-6480
            800-769-6199

T   Trellis Books
            c/o Fahy-Williams Publishing, Inc.
            P.O. Box 1080
            171 Reed Street
            Geneva, NY 14456
            800-344-0559

WA   Ward's
            P.O. Box 92912
            Rochester, NY 14692-9012
            800-962-2660

WP   Watten Poe Teaching Resource Center
            P.O. Box 1509
            San Leandro, CA 94577
            800-833-3389

W   The Writing Company
            Division of Social Studies School Service
            10200 Jefferson Boulevard, Room WR2
            P.O. Box 802
            Culver City, CA 90232-0802
            800-421-4246

Z   Zephyr Press
            3316 N. Chapel Ave.
            P.O. Box 13448-C
            Tucson, AZ 85732-3448
            602-322-5090

Chapter Fifteen

Media/Instructional Materials Sources by Type

Below is a list of sources of media and instructional materials arranged by material type. The producer or distributor appearing under each format is abbreviated; the abbreviations and the addresses for the companies they represent appear in chapter 17.

Audio Compact Discs

GLE, HOL, HOU, IND, KIM, MAC, NYS, SIL, TIM

Audiocassettes

ADD, AMEG, AMES, AUD, BOOK, CARO, CARS, COMS, CONT, CRET, EDC, EDUCA, EDUCI, FIL, GLE, GLO, HAL, HAR, HEAT, HOL, HOU, IDE, IND, JAB, JAN, KIM, MODC, MODT, NATS, NOV, PER, PRE, S&S, SCOF, SIL, SOC, SPO, SRA, SUM, SUND, TIM, WES

Awards

BAU, CARS, CREE, ETA, FRA, INS, JUD, MEDM, NAS, TRE

Book/Cassettes

AWP, ADD, AME, CUR, EDUCI, GLO, GRA, HPK, HAR, HOT, HOU, JAB, JAN, KIM, MODC, NYS, PER, SPO, SUND, WES

Bulletin Board Sets

CARS, CREE, FRA, TRE

Card Sets

AMEG, COMS, CREP, CRET, DID, ECS, EDUCI, FRA, HAR, IDE, JUD, MEDM, MODC, SIL, SRA, TRE, VIS

CD-ROMs

AIMSM, BER, BRI, CAMD, CARO, CARS, CONN, CORP, CREC, DAV, DID, DIS, EDC, EDUCA, EDUCR, EME, FIL, GAM, GLO, HEA, HEAT, HOU, JAN, KIM, KNO, LIB, MAC, MEC, MIL, MODC, MODT, NAS, NATG, NATS, OPT, ORA, QUE, SAR, SCI, SCOF, SIL, SOC, SOCIET, SOF, SUNB, TIG, TIM, VID, WAR, WRI, ZEN, ZTE

Charts

AMEG (pocket), CARO, CARS, CONN, CREE, CRET, CUI, DEN, ETA, FRA, HAM, HAR, HEA, HOU, HUB, JUD, KNO, NAS, NATG, NATS, NYS, POS, SAR, SCI, SIL, SOC, TRE, WAR, WAT (pocket), WRI

Computer Programs

ADD, AIMSM, BAU, BRO, CAMD, CARO, CHA, CONN, CREC, CRI, CUR, DAV, DID, DIS, EDM, EDUCA, EDUCR, EME, GAM, GLE, HAR, HEA, HEAT, HOL, HOU, HUM, JOS, LAU, MAC, MEC, MIL, MIN, MODT, NAS, NATS, ORA, SAR, SCH, SCI, SCOR, SIL, SOC, SOCIET, SOF, SRA, SUM, SUNB, TEACHE, TOM, WAR, WFF, WRI, ZEN

Displays

CARO, CONN, HEA, NAS, NATS, SAR, SCI, TRE

Equipment and Supplies (Curriculum-Oriented)

AIMSE, CARO, CONN, CUI, DEL, DID, ETA, HUB, IDE, NAS, PER, S&S, SAR, SCI, WAR, WAT

File Folder Activities

EDU

Films

DISN, DOCE, FILMI, MODT, ROL, WES

Filmstrips

AWP, AMES, COMC, KIM, KNO, MODT, NAS, NATG, NYS, PIE, SAR, SIL, SOC, SOCIET, SPO, WES

Flannel Board Visuals

JUD, MEDM

Flash Cards

CREE, CRET, DID, ETA, FRA, HAL, IDE, MEDM, MILT, NAS, SOC, SUM, TRE

Game Pieces For Making Games

CRET, CUI, DEL, ETA, IDE, MEDM, MILT, SUM

Games

CARO, COMS, CONN, CREE, CREP, CRET, CUI, DEL, DID, EDUCA, EDUCI, ETA, FIL, FRA, HAL, HEA, HOU, HUB, IDE, JUD, KID, MEDM, MILT, MODC, NAS, NATS, S&S, SCI, SCOR, SIM, SOC, SRA, SUNB, TRE, WAR, WFF, WRI

Globes

CRA, DEL, HUB, NYS, SAR, SCI

Kits

ADD, AIMSE, AMEG, COMS, CONN, CONT, CRA, CREP, CRET, CUI, DEL, DID, ECS, EDUCI, ETA, ETH, GRA, HPK, HAR, HEAT, HOU, HUB, IDE, JAC, JUD, LEG, MAC, MODC, NAS, NYS, PER, S&S, SAR, SCI, SCOR, SIL, SRA, SUM, SUNB, THE, WAR, ZAN

Magnetic Board Visuals

CUI, EDUCI, JUD, SAR, STE

Manipulatives

AIMSE, CARS, CREE, CREP, CRET, CUI, DEL, DID, EDUCI, ETA, HAR, HEAT, IDE, JUD, MAC, MEDM, MODC, NAS, SAR, SCOR, SIL, SRA, SUM, TEACHL, WAR, WAT

Maps

CRA, DID, GRA, HAM, HUB, JUD, KNO, MODC, NATG, NYS, SAR, SIL

Models

AWP (children's literature), CARO, CONN, DEL, DEN, EDUCI, ETA, HEA, HUB, NAS, NATS, NYS, SAR, SCI, SOC, WAR, WES (children's literature)

Overhead Manipulatives

AIMSE, CARS, CREE, CREP, CRET, CUI, DEL, DID, ETA, HAR, HEAT, HOU, IDE, JUS, MAC, MODC, NAS, SCOR, SIL, SUM, WAT

Overhead Transparencies

ADD, CONN, DEN, GLE, GLO, HAM, HAR, HEA, HEAT, HOL, HOU, HUB, LEG, MAC, MIL, MODC, NAS, NATS, NYS, PRE, SAR, SCI, SCOF, SIL, SOC, UNI

Pamphlets

KID, NATS, SOC

Pictures

AMEG, COMS, CREE, CREP, DAL, DID, DOCP, FRA, GLE, GRA, HAR, HOU, HUB, IDE, JUD, KNO, MEDM, ML, MODC, NAS, NYS, POS, SAR, SIL, SOC, SRA, THE, TRE

Plays

CRET, CUR, EDUCI, INC, JWES, MIL, NATS

Posters

AWP, CARO, CONN, CREE, CREP, DOCP, ECS, FRA, HAR, HEA, HOL, HOU, IDE, INS, JUD, KNO, MEDM, MODC, NATS, PER, POS, SAR, SCI, SIL, SOC, SRA, SUNB, TRE, WAR, WRI

Puppets

CARS, MAH, NAN, ONE, PUP, SRA, SUNB

Puzzles

CREE, DID, FRA, JUD, MODC, S&S

Realia/Artifacts/Facsimiles

ETH, JAC, NAS, SAR, EDUCA, IND, KIM, MAC, S&S, SIL

Slides—Microscope

CARO, CONN, NAS, SAR, SCI, WAR

Slides—Regular

AMEL, DAL, HEAT, HUB, NAS, WAR

Teaching Clocks

CREP, CRET, DEL, DID, EDUCI, ETA, IDE, JUD, MEDM, MODC, SRA

Videocassettes

AWP, ADD, AGE, ALT, AMEG, AMES, BAK, BER, BO, BRI, CAMS, CARO, CHI, CONN, CORO, COY, CREL, CREP, DEL, DID, DISN, DOCE, EDC, EDUCA, EDUCV, EME, ETA, ETR, FIL, FILMH, FILMI, GLE, GLO, GRE, HPK, HAR, HAW, HEA, HEAT, HIG, HOL, HOT, HOU, HRM, HUB, INST, JAB, JAN, KID, KIM, KNO, LEA, LIB, MAC, MEDB, MODC, MODT, MOV, NAS, NAEYC, NCTE, NCTM, NATG, NATS, NSTA, NEW, NOV, NYS, PBS, PER, PIE, RAI, ROL, SAR, SCI, SCO, SCOR, SIG, SIL, SOC, SOCIET, SPO, SRA, SUNB, SUND, TIM, TVO, WAR, WES, WRI, ZEN

Videodiscs

ADD, AIMSM, ALT, BRI, CARO, CONN, CORO, CREC, EDUCA,
EDUCR, EME, FIL, GLE, GLO, HAR, HEAT, HOL, HOU, MAC,
MODC, MODT, NATG, OPT, PEG, PIE, PRE, SAR, SCOF, SCOR,
SIL, SOC, SOCIET, SUNB, VID, WAR, ZEN, ZTE

Vinyl Cling-On Visuals

EDUCI, INS

Chapter Sixteen

Media/Instructional Materials Sources by Curriculum Area

This list is arranged alphabetically by curriculum area with the various formats available listed under each area. The producer or distributor appearing under each format is abbreviated; the abbreviations and the addresses for the companies they represent appear in chapter 17.

Art

CD-ROMs
CREC, LIB, MODT, QUE

Computer Programs
EDUCR, NAS

Equipment and Supplies
NAS, S&S

Films
FILMI, ROL

Filmstrips
AME, COMC, NAS

Games

NAS

Kits

S & S

Overhead Transparencies

GLE, HAR, NAS

Pictures

DAL, DID, GLE, HAR, KNO, NAS, SOS

Posters

KNO

Slides

AMEL, DAL, NAS

Videocassettes

AGE, AME, BRI, COY, EDUCV, FILMH, FILMI, INST, KNO, LIB,
MEDR, MODT, NAS, PIE, RAI, ROL, TVO, ZEN

Videodiscs

CREC, SOCIET, VID, ZEN, ZIE

Basic Skills

Audiocassettes

EDUCA, EDUCI

Card Sets

MEDM

CD-ROMs
BER, QUE

Charts
FRA

Computer Programs
CREC, LAU, QUE

Kits
AMEG

Records
EDUCA

Videocassettes
BER, EDUCA

Critical Thinking Skills

Audiocassettes
EDUCA

CD-ROMs
CAMD, CREC, SUNB

Computer Software
CAMD, CREC, CRI, EDM, SUNB

Games
WFF

Posters
SOC

English as a Second Language

Audiocassettes
ADD, JAB

Books/Cassettes
CUR, GRA, JAB, SPO

Charts
WAT

Computer Programs
HUM, JOS, SCH

Kits
GRA

Magnetic Board Visuals
STE

Posters
HAR

Videocassettes
NATS, SPO

Foreign Language

Audio Compact Discs
HOL, HOU

Audiocassettes
CARS, GLE, HEAT, HOL, HOU, JAB, KIM, MODC, SCOF, SPO

Books/Cassettes
AWP, HOT, SPO

Card Sets
MEDM, VIS

CD-ROMs
CREC, HEAT, KIM, QUE, SCOF, TIG

Charts
FRA

Computer Programs
CREC, EDUCR, HOU, MODT, NATS, SOF

Flannel Board Visuals
MEDM

Flash Cards
MEDM, TRE

Overhead Transparencies
HEAT, HOL, SCOF

Pictures
HOU, ML

Posters
INS

Videocassettes
AMES, BAK, BRI, CORO, EDUCV, FILMH, GLE, HEAT, HOL, HOU, INST, KIM, MEDB, MODT, NATS, SCOF, SPO, TVO

Videodiscs

BRI, CORP, GLE, HEAT, HOL, SCOF, ZTE

Graphics and Publishing

Computer Software

BAU, BRO, CAMD, CREC, DAV, EDUCR, NATS, SCH, SOF, TEACHE

Guidance

CD-ROMs

BER

Filmstrips

AMES, MODT, PIE

Games

KID, SIM, SUNB

Kits

AMEG, SUNB

Pamphlets

KID

Posters

SUNB

Videocassettes

AWP, ALT, AMEG, BAK, BER, BRI, CREL, DISN, EDC, EDUCV, ETR, FILMH, HRM, INST, JAN, KID, LEA, MEDB, MODT, PBS, PIE, RAI, SUNB, ZEN

Videodiscs
AIMSM

Health

Audiocassettes
EDUCA, GLE, MODC, NATS, S&S

Bulletin Board Sets
TRE

CD-ROMs
CREC, EDUCR, HEA, HEAT, QUE

Charts
CRET, DEN, FRA, HEA, JUD, NATS, TRE

Computer Programs
CREC, HEA, EDUCR

Displays
HEA, NATS

Films
DISN, FILMI, MODT

Filmstrips
AMES, NYS, SOCIET

Flannel Board Visuals
JUD

Flash Cards
TRE

Games
CRET, HEA, NATS, SUNB

Kits
AMEG, SRA, SUNB

Models
NATS

Overhead Transparencies
GLE, HEA, HEAT, HOL, NATS

Pamphlets
NATS

Plays
NATS

Posters
HEA, IDE, NATS

Puppets
SUNB

Records
EDUCA, S&S

Videocassettes
AWP, AGE, ALT, AME, BAK, BRI, CORO, DISN, EDUCA,
EDUCV, FILMH, FILMI, GLE, HEA, HOT, HRM, INST, LEA, LIB,
MEDB, MODT, NATS, PBS, PIE, RAI, SIG, SUNB, TVO, ZEN

Videodiscs
AIMSM, BRI, CORO, CREC, HEAT, MODC, MODT, PEG,
SOCIET

Language Arts

Audiocassettes

CARS, COMS, EDC, EDUCA, GLE, HEAT, IDE, MODC, SIL

Books/Cassettes

EDUCI, SPO

Bulletin Board Sets

FRA, TRE

Card Sets

AMEG, COMS, CRET, DID, EDUCI, FRA, HAR, IDE, JUD,
MEDM, MODC, SRA, TRE, VIS

CD-ROMs

CAMS, CREC, DAV, EDUCR, FIL, LIB, MAC, MIL, NATS, ORA,
QUE, SOCIET, SOF, SUNB, TIG, WRI, ZTE

Charts

FRA, HAR, HOU, JUD, TRE, WRI

Computer Programs

BRO, CAMD, CHA, CREC, CUR, DAV, DISK, EDM, EDUCA,
EDUCR, GAM, GLE, HAR, HOL, HOU, HUM, JOS, LAU, MEC,
MIL, MIN, NATS, ORA, SCH, SIL, SOCIET, SRA, SUNB,
TEACHE, TOM, WRI

Films

DISN, FILMI

Filmstrips

AMES, COMC, KNO, NATG, NYS, PIE, SOCIET, SPO

Flannel Board Visuals

JUD

Flash Cards

CREE, FRA, IDE, MEDM, MILT, TRE

Games

COMS, CREE, CRET, DID, EDUCA, FRA, IDE, JUD, MEDM, MILT, SRA, TRE, WFF, WRI

Kits

AMEG, CONT, HAR, MODC, SIL, SRA, THE

Magnetic Board Visuals

EDUCI, STE

Overhead Transparencies

GLE, GLO, HAR, HEAT, HOL, HOU, SCOF, SIL, UNI

Pictures

COMS, DAL, SRA, THE

Plays

CUR, EDUCI, INC

Posters

HOU, KNO, MODC, SOC, WRI

Videocassettes

AWP, AGE, ALT, BAK, BRI, CHI, CORO, DISN, EDC, EDUCA, EDUCV, FIL, FILMH, FILMI, CLE, GRE, HEAT, HRM, INST, JAN, KNO, LIB, MEDB, MODT, NATG, NATS, NYS, PBS, PIE, RAI, SIG, SIL, SOCIET, SPO, SUND, TVO, WRI, ZEN, AIMSM, CREC, EDUCA, EDUCR, GLE, HAR, HOU, SOCIET, ZEN, ZTE

Literature—Children's

Audiocassettes

AMES, BOOK, EDC, HAR, HEAT, HOU, JAB, JAN, NOV, PER, SIL, SPO, SUND, WES

Books/Cassettes

AWP, ADD, AMES, GRA, HAR, HOT, HOU, JAB, JAN, KIM, MODC, NYS, PER, SPO, SUND, WES

CD-ROMs

CREC, DIS, DIS, EDUCR, HOU, LIB, MAC, NATS, ORA, QUE, SIL, SOCIET, SOF, TIG, ZTE

Computer Programs

EDUCR, HUM, ORA

Films

DISN, FILMI, WES

Filmstrips

AWP, AMES, KIM, PIE, SOCIET, WES

Flannel Board Visuals

MEDM, JUD

Kits

GRA, HPK, PER, ZAN

Magnetic Board Visuals

STE

Models (Plush Literature Characters)

AWP, WES

Pictures

GRA

Plays

MIL

Posters

AWP, PER, SRA

Videocassettes

AWP, AGE, AMES, BAK, BRI, CHI, CORO, CREL, DISN, FIL, FILMI, HPK, HOT, INST, JAB, KIM, KNO, LIB, MEDB, MODT, MOV, NOV, PBS, PER, PIE, SIL, SOCIET, SPO, SRA, SUND, WES, ZEN

Videodiscs

AIMSM, CORO, HOU, SIL, ZTE

Literature—Young Adult

Audiocassettes

AMES, AUD, BOOK, CONT, FIL, GLE, GLO, HEAT, HOL, JAB, NOV, PER, SCOF, SPO

Books/Cassettes

EDUCI, GLO, HPK, JAB

Card Sets

EDUCI

CD-ROMs

EDUCR, FIL, JAN, QUE

Computer Programs

HUM

Kits

CONT, ECS, HPK, PER

Films

FILMI

Filmstrips

AMES, MODT

Overhead Transparencies

SCOF

Posters

HOL, PER

Videocassettes

BAK, BRI, CHI, CORO, CREL, FIL, FILMH, FILMI, GLE, GLO, HPK, JAB, JAN, KNO, LIB, MEDB, MODT, MOV, NOV, PBS, PER, SUND, WRI, ZEN

Videodiscs

BRI, FIL, ZEN, ZTE

Mathematics

Audio Compact Discs

EDUCA

Audiocassettes

CARS, CRET, EDC, EDUCA, SUM

Bulletin Board Sets

FRA, TRE

Card Sets

CREP, CRET, ECS, FRA, IDE, JUD, MEDM, TRE, VIS

CD-ROMs

CAMD, CREC, DAV, EDC, EDUCR, GAM, HEAT, LIB, MODC, ORA, TIG

Charts

FRA, TRE

Computer Programs

ADD, BRO, CAMD, CHA, CREC, CUR, DAV, DID, DISK, EDM, EDUCA, EDUCR, GAM, GLE, HAR, HEAT, HOU, JOS, MEC, MIL, MIN, NAS, NATS, ORA, SCH, SCOR, SIL, SOCIET, SOF, SRA, SUM, SUNB, TOM, WFF

Equipment and Supplies

AIMSE, CUI, ETA, NAS

Films

DISN, FILMI

Filmstrips

NATG, SOCIET

Flannel Board Visuals

JUD, MEDM

Flash Cards

CREE, CRET, DID, ETA, FRA, IDE, MEDM, MILT, NAS, SUM, TRE

Games

CREE, CREP, CRET, CUI, DEL, DID, EDUCI, ETA, FRA, HOU, IDE, JUD, MEDM, MODC, NAS, SCOR, SRA, TRE, WFF

Kits

ADD, AIMSE, CONT, CREP, CUI, DID, ETA, HAR, HEAT, HOU, JUD, MAC, NAS, NATS, PIE, SIL, SOCIET, TVO

Magnetic Board Visuals

CUI, JUD, STE

Manipulatives

AIMSE, CARS, CREE, CREP, CRET, CUI, DEL, DID, EDUCI, ETA, HAR, HEAT, IDE, JUD, MAC, MODC, NAS, SCOR, SIL, SRA, SUM, TEACHL, WAT

Overhead Manipulatives

AIMSE, CARS, CREE, CREP, CRET, CUI, DEL, DID, ETA, HAR, HEAT, HOU, IDE, MAC, MODC, NAS, SCOR, SIL, SUM, WAT

Overhead Transparencies

ADD, GLE, HEAT, HOL, HOU, MAC, MIL, SIL, UNI

Pictures

DAL

Posters

CREP, ECS

Records

EDUCA

Teaching Clocks

CREP, CRET, DEL, DID, EDUCI, ETA, IDE, JUD, MEDM, MODC, SRA

Videocassettes

AGE, ALT, BAK, BRI, CORO, CREP, DISN, EDC, ETA, FILMI, GRE, HOT, HRM, INST, LIB, MEDB, MODC, MODT, NAS, NATS, PIE, SIL, SOCIET, TVO

Videodiscs

AIMSM, ALT, CORO, CREC, HEAT, OPT, SOCIET, VID

Music

Audio Compact Discs

EDUCA, GLE, IND, KIM, MAC, SIL, TIM

Audiocassettes

CONT, EDUCA, GLE, HAL, HOU, IND, KIM, MODC, PER, S&S, SIL, SPO, SRA, TIM

Books/Cassettes

CUR

Bulletin Board Sets

FRA, TRE

CD-ROMs

CREC, LIB, ORA, QUE, SOF, SUNB, ZTE

Charts

SIL

Computer Programs

CREC, EDUCR, MAC, NATS, SCH, SIL

Equipment and Supplies

S&S

Films

DISN, FILMI

Filmstrips

AMES

Flash Cards

HAL

Games

HAL

Overhead Transparencies

SIL, UNI

Pictures

SIL

Plays

MIL

Records

EDUCA, IND, KIM, MAC, S&S, SIL

Videocassettes

AGE, BRI, CORO, DISN, EDUCA, EDUCV, FILMI, INST, JAB, KIM, LIB, MAC, MEDB, MODT, SIL, SOCIET, TIM, TVO, ZEN

Videodiscs

BRI, ZTE

Preschool

Audio Compact Discs

KIM

Audiocassettes

EDUCA, HAL, KIM, MODC, S&S, SRA

Bulletin Board Sets

CREE, FRA, TRE

Card Sets

COMS, DID, JUD, MEDM, MODC, SRA, TRE

CD-ROMs

CAMD, CREC, DIS, DISK, EDUCR, LIB, NATS, OPT, ORA, SOCIET, SUNB, TIG

Charts

FRA, JUD, TRE, WAT

Computer Programs

BRO, CAMD, CHA, CREC, DAV, DISK, EDM, EDUCA, EDUCR, GAM, JOS, LAU, MAC, MIN, NATS, ORA, SCH, SOCIET, SOF, SUNB

Filmstrips

AMES, SOCIET

Flannel Board Kits

JUD

Flash Cards

MILT

Games

DID, MEDM, S&S

Kits

AMEG, COMS, HEAT, HOU, MODC, SIL, SRA, ZAN

Manipulatives
DID, SRA

Pictures
COMS, JUD, THE

Posters
MODC

Puzzles
CREE, DID, FRA, JUD, MODC, S&S

Records
EDUCA, KIM, S&S

Videocassettes
EDUCA, HOT, KIM, LIB, MEDB, NATS, SOCIET

Videodiscs
CREC, OPT, SOCIET

Professional Education

Videocassettes
AGE, ETA, FILMH, HIG, NAEYC, NCTE, NCTM, NSTA, PBS, SUNB

Videodiscs
OPT

Reference

CD-ROMs
AIMSM, BRI, CREC, DAV, EDUCR, FIL, LIB, MODT, NATG, NATS, SOC, SOCIET, SUNB, TIG, ZTE

Computer Programs

BRO, EDUCR, MODT

Science

Audio Compact Discs

CARO, NYS

Audiocassettes

CARO

Books/Cassettes

NYS

Bulletin Board Sets

CREE, FRA, TRE

Card Sets

FRA, JUD, MEDM, TRE, VIS

CD-ROMs

AIMSM, CAMD, CARO, CARS, CONN, CREC, DAV, DID, DISN,
EDUCA, EDUCR, EME, GAM, GLO, HEA, LIB, MODT, NAS,
NATG, NATS, ORA, QUE, SAR, SCI, SOCIET, SOF, SUNB, TIG,
TIM, VID, WAR, ZTE

Charts

CARO, CONN, CUI, DEN, ETA, FRA, HEA, HUB, JUD, KNO,
NAS, NATG, NYS, POS, SAR, SCI, TRE, WAR

Computer Programs

AIMSM, BRO, CAMD, CARO, CHA, CONN, CREC, DAV, DISK,
EDM, EDUCA, EDUCR, EME, GAM, GLE, HEAT, JOS, MEC,
MIN, NATS, ORA, SAR, SCH, SCI, SIL, SOCIET, SOF, SUNB,
TOM, WAR

Displays

CARO, CONN, NAS, SAR, SCI, TRE

Equipment and Supplies

CARO, CONN, CUI, DEL, DID, ETA, HUB, IDE, NAS, SAR, SCI, WAR

Films

DISN, FILMI, MODT

Filmstrips

AMES, KNO, MODT, NATG, NYS, PIE, SAR, SIL, SOCIET

Flannel Board Visuals

JUD

Flash Cards

IDE, TRE

Games

CARO, CONN, DEL, ETA, HUB, MILT, NAS, SCI, WAR

Kits

ADD, AIMSE, CARO, CONN, CREP, CRET, CUI, DEL, DID, EDUCI, ETA, HPK, HAR, HUB, IDE, JUD, LEG, NAS, NYS, SAR, SCI, SCOR, SIL, SUM, WAR

Magnetic Board Visuals

SAR, STE

Manipulatives

ETA, SAR, WAR

Models

CARO, CONN, DEL, DEN, EDUCI, ETA, HEA, HUB, NAS, NYS, SAR, SCI, WAR

Overhead Manipulatives

DID

Overhead Transparencies

ADD, CONN, DEN, GLE, GLO, HEA, HEAT, HOL, HUB, LEG, MAC, MIL, NAS, SAR, SCI, SIL, UNI

Pictures

CREE, CREP, DAL, DID, DOCP, FRA, HUB, IDE, JUD, MEDM, NAS, NYS, SAR, TRE

Posters

CARO, CONN, CREE, DOCP, IDE, INS, JUD, KNO, MODC, POS, SAR, SCI, SIL, WAR

Puzzles

CREE, FRA, JUD

Realia

NAS, SAR

Slides—Microscope

CARO, CONN, NAS, SAR, SCI, WAR

Slides—Regular

CARO, CONN, HUB, WAR

Videocassettes

AWP, ADD, AGE, ALT, AMEG, BAK, BO, BRI, CARO, CHI, CONN, CORO, DEL, DID, DISN, EDC, EDUCA, EDUCV, EME,

ETA, FILMH, FILMI, GLE, GLO, GRE, HAR, HAW, HEA, HEAT, HOL, HOT, HUB, INS, JAN, KIM, KNO, LIB, MAC, MEDB, MODC, MODT, NAS, NATG, NATS, NYS, PBS, PIE, RAI, SAR, SCI, SCOR, SIG, SIL, SOCIET, TIM, TVO, WAR, ZEN

Videodiscs

ADD, AIMSM, ALT, BRI, CARO, CONN, CORO, CREC, EDUCR, EME, GLE, GLO, HEAT, HOL, MAC, MODC, MODT, NATG, OPT, PEG, PIE, SAR, SCOR, SIL, SOCIET, SUNB, VID

Vinyl Cling-On Visuals

EDUCI

Social Studies

Audio Compact Discs

IND

Audiocassettes

CARS, FIL, HEAT, HOL, HOU, IND, PRE, SIL, SOC

Books/Cassettes

CUR, NYS, SPO

Bulletin Board Sets

CREE, FRA, TRE

Card Sets

FRA, JUD, MEDM, SIL, TRE, VIS

Charts

CREE, FRA, HAM, JUD, KNO, POS, SOC, TRE

CD-ROMs

CAMD, CREC, DAV, EDUCR, FIL, GAM, GLO, HEAT, HOU, KNO, LIB, MEC, MODT, NATG, NATS, ORA, QUE, SOC, SOF, TIG, ZEN, ZTE

Computer Programs

AIMSM, BRO, CAMD, CHA, CREC, DAV, DISK, EDUCA, EDUCR, GAM, MEC, NATS, ORA, SCH, SOC, SOCIET, SOF, SUNB, TOM, ZEN

Displays

TRE

Films

DISN, DOCE, FILMI, MODT

Filmstrips

AMES, KNO, MODT, NATG, NYS, SOC, SOCIET, SPO

Flannel Board Visuals

JUD

Flash Cards

MEDM, SOC, TRE

Games

CRET, DID, EDUCI, FIL, MILT, SIM, SOC, TRE, WFF

Globes

CRA, DEL, HUB, NYS, SAR, SCI

Kits

CRA, ETH, HEAT, JAC, NYS, SOC, SRA

Magnetic Board Visuals

STE

Maps—Desk

CRA, GRA, HAM, MODC, NYS, SIL

Maps—Floor

DID, NYS

Maps—Puzzle

JUD, MODC

Maps—Wall

CRA, HUB, KNO, MODC, NATG, NYS, POS, SAR

Models

NYS, SOC

Overhead Transparencies

ADD, GLE, GLO, HAM, HAR, HEAT, HOL, HOU, HUB, MIL, MODC, NYS, PRE, SIL, SOC

Pamphlets

SOC

Pictures

AMEG, CREE, DOCP, GRA, HAR, HOU, IDE, JUD, MEDM, MODC, NYS, POS, SOC, TRE

Plays

CUR, JWES

Posters

CREE, HOU, INS, JUD, KNO, MEDM, MODC, POS, SOC

Puzzles

CREE, DID, JUD, MODC

Realia/Artifacts/Facsimiles

ETH, JAC, SOC

Records

IND

Slides

HEAT

Videocassettes

AWP, AGE, ALT, BAK, BRI, CAMS, CHI, CORO, DISN, DOCE, EDUCV, FIL, FILMH, FILMI, GLE, GRE, HAW, HEAT, HOL, HOT, INST, JAB, JAN, KIM, KNO, LIB, MEDB, MODT, NATG, NATS, NEW, NYS, PBS, PIE, RAI, SIG, SIL, SOC, SOCIET, SPO, TVO, ZEN

Videodiscs

AIMSM, ALT, BRI, CORO, CREC, EDUCR, FIL, GLE, GLO, HEAT, HOL, HOU, MAC, NATG, PIE, PRE, SIL, SOC, SOCIET, VID, ZEN, ZTE

Study Skills

Audiocassettes

AMEG, EDUCA

Computer Programs

NATS

Videocassettes

BAK, EDC, EDUCV, MODT, NATS, ZEN

Teacher Utility Computer Software

Computer Programs

BRO, CREC, DAV, DISK, EDM, EDUCR, MIN, NATS, SCH, TEACHE

Vocational

Audiocassettes

EDC, MODT

CD-ROMs

BER, CREC, QUE

Computer Programs

MODT

Filmstrips

AMES, MODT

Overhead Transparencies

UNI

Videocassettes

BAK, BER, EDUCV, FILMH, GLE, HRM, INST, MODT, TVO, ZEN

Chapter Seventeen

Media/Instructional Materials Producer and Distributor Sources

AWP	A.W. Peller & Associates, Inc. 210 Sixth Avenue P.O. Box 106 Hawthorne, NJ 07607-0106 973-423-4666
ADD	Addison-Wesley 2725 Sand Hill Road Menlo, CA 94025 415-854-0300
AGE	Agency for Instructional Technology Box A Bloomington, IN 47402-2203 800-457-4509
AIMSE	AIMS Education Foundation P.O. Box 8120 Fresno, CA 93747-8120 209-255-4094
AIMSM	AIMS Media 9710 DeSoto Avenue Chatsworth, CA 91311-4409 800-367-2467
ALT	Altschul Group Corporation 1560 Sherman Avenue Suite #100 Evanston, IL 60201 800-323-9084

AMEG   American Guidance Service
                    4201 Woodland Road
                    P.O. Box 99
                    Circle Pines, MN 55014-1796
                    800-328-2560

AMEL   American Library Color Slide Co., Inc.
                    American Archives of World Art
                    P.O. Box 4414
                    Grand Central Station
                    New York, NY 10163-4414
                    800-633-3307

AMES   American School Publishers
                    155 North Wacker Drive
                    P.O. Box 4520
                    Chicago, IL 60680-4520
                    800-843-8855

AUD   Audio Book Contractors, Inc.
                    Classic Books on Cassettes
                    P.O. Box 40115
                    Washington, DC 20016-0115

BAK   Baker & Taylor
                    P.O. Box 734
                    Somerville, NJ 08876-0734
                    800-775-1800

BAU   Baudville
                    5380 52nd Street, S.E.
                    Grand Rapids, MI 49512-9765
                    800-728-0888

BER   Bergwall Productions, Inc.
                    540 Baltimore Pike
                    P.O. Box 2400
                    Chadds Ford, PA 19317-9304
                    800-645-3565

BO   Bo Peep Productions
                    P.O. Box 982
                    Eureka, MT 59917
                    800-532-0420

BOOK   Books on Tape, Inc.
              P.O. Box 7900
              Newport Beach, CA 92658
              800-626-3333

BRI   Britannica
              310 South Michigan Avenue
              Chicago, IL 60604-9839
              800-554-9862

BRO   Broderbund
              Dept. 93EC
              P.O. Box 6125
              Novato, CA 04948-6125
              415-382-4400

CAMD   Cambridge Development Laboratory, Inc.
              86 West Street
              Waltham, MA 02154
              800-637-0047

CAMS   Cambridge Social Studies
              P.O. Box 2153
              Dept. SS6
              Charleston, WV 25328-2153
              800-468-4227

CARO   Carolina Biological Supply Co.
              2700 York Road
              Burlington, NC 27215
              800-334-5551

CARS   Carson-Dellosa Publishing Company, Inc.
              P.O. Box 35665
              Greensboro, NC 27425
              910-632-0084

CHA   Chariot Software Group
              3659 India Street
              Suite 100E
              San Diego, CA 92103
              800-242-7468

CHI Children's Television International
14512A Lee Road
Chantilly, VA 22021
800-CTI-GLAD

COMC Communicad
The Communications Academy
Box 541R
Wilton, CT 06897
800-762-7464

COMS Communication Skill Builders
A Division of The Psychological Corporation
555 Academic Court
San Antonio, TX 78204-2498
800-228-0752

CONN Connecticut Valley Biological
82 Valley Road
P.O. Box 326
Southampton, MA 01073
413-527-4030

CONT Continental Press
520 E. Bainbridge Street
Elizabeth, PA 17022
1-800-233-0759

CORO Coronet MTI
4350 Equity Drive
P.O. BOX 2649
Columbus, OH 43216-2649
800-321-3106

COY Coyote Creek Productions
2419 East Mission Road
Fallbrook, CA 92028
619-731-3184

CRA George F. Cram Company, Inc.
P.O. Box 426
Indianapolis, IN 46206
800-227-4199

CREC	Creative Computer Visions 3324 Pennsylvania Avenue Charleston, WV 25302 304-346-4292
CREE	Creative Educational Materials P.O. Box 18127 West St. Paul, MN 55118-0127 800-888-2343
CREL	Creative Learning P.O. Box 134 Saunderstown, RI 02874 800-542-2468
CREP	Creative Publications 5623 W. 115th Street Worth, IL 60482-9931 800-624-0822
CRET	Creative Teaching Associates P.O. Box 7766 Fresno, CA 93747 800-767-4282
CRI	Critical Thinking Books & Software P.O. Box 448 Pacific Grove, CA 93950-0448 800-458-4849
CUI	Cuisenaire Co. of America, Inc. P.O. Box 5026 White Plains, NY 10602-5026 800-237-0338
CUR	Curriculum Associates, Inc. 5 Esquire Road P.O. Box 2001 N. Billerica, MA 01862-0901 508-667-8000
DAL	Dale Seymour Publications P.O. Box 10888 Palo Alto, CA 94303-0879 800-827-1100

DAV   Davidson & Associates, Inc.
             P.O. Box 2961
             Torrance, CA 90509
             800-545-7677

DEL   Delta Education
             P.O. Box 3000
             Nashua, NH 03061-3000
             800-442-5444

DEN   Denoyer-Geppert International
             5225 Ravenswood Avenue
             Chicago, IL 60640-2028
             312-561-9200

DID   Didax
             395 Main Street
             Rowley, MA 01969-3785
             800-458-0024

DIS   Discis Knowledge Research, Inc.
             P.O. Box 66
             Buffalo, NY 14223-0066
             800-567-4321

DISK   Diskovery Educational Systems
             1860 Old Okeechobee Road, Suite 106
             West Palm Beach, FL 33409
             800-331-5489

DISN   Disney Educational Productions
             108 Wilmot Road
             Deerfield, IL 60015
             800-621-2131

DOCE   Documentary Educational Resources
             101 Morse Street
             Watertown, MA 02172
             617-926-0491

DOCP   Documentary Photo Aids
             P.O. Box 956
             Mt. Dora, FL 32757
             800-255-0763

ECS   ECS Learning Systems, Inc.
P.O. Box 791437
San Antonio, TX 78279-1437
800-68-TEACH

EDC   EDCON Publishing Group
30 Montauk Boulevard
Oakdale, NY 11769
516-567-7227

EDM   EDMARK
P.O. Box 97021
Redmond, WA 98073-9721
800-362-2890

EDU   The Education Center, Inc.
P.O. Box 9753
1607 Battleground Avenue
Greensboro, NC 27429
800-334-0298

EDUCA   Educational Activities, Inc.
P.O. Box 392
Freeport, NY 11520
800-645-3739

EDUCI   Educational Insights
19560 South Rancho Way
Dominguez Hills, CA 90220
310-884-1931

EDUCR   Educational Resources
Box 1900
1550 Executive Drive
Elgin, IL 60121-1900
800-624-2926

EDUCV   Educational Video Network
1490 19th Street
Huntsville, TX 77340
800-762-0060

EME   EME Corporation
P.O. Box 2805
Danbury, CT 06813-2805
800-848-2050

ETA   ETA
                   620 Lakeview Parkway
                   Vernon Hills, IL 60061
                   800-445-5985

ETH   Ethnic Arts & Facts
                   P.O. Box 20550
                   Oakland, CA 94620
                   510-465-0451

ETR   ETR Associates
                   P.O. Box 1830
                   Santa Cruz, CA 95061-1830
                   408-438-4060

FIL   Filmic Archives
                   The Cinema Center
                   Botsford, CT 06404-0386
                   800-366-1920

FILMH   Films for the Humanities & Sciences
                   P.O. Box 2053
                   Princeton, NJ 08543-2053
                   800-257-5126

FILMI   Films Incorporated Video
                   5547 N. Ravenswood Avenue
                   Chicago, IL 60640-1199
                   800-323-4222

FRA   Frank Schaffer Publications, Inc.
                   23740 Hawthorne Boulevard
                   P.O. Box 2853
                   Torrance, CA 90509-2853
                   800-421-5565

GAM   GAMCO Education Materials
                   P.O. Box 1911M12
                   Big Springs, TX 79721-1911
                   800-351-1404

GLE   Glencoe
                   P.O. Box 508
                   Columbus, OH 43216
                   800-334-7344

GLO	Globe Prentice Hall 4350 Equity Drive P.O. Box 2649 Columbus, OH 43216 800-848-9500
GRA	Graphic Learning A Division of ABRAMS & COMPANY Publishers, Inc. 61 Mattatuck Heights Road Waterbury, CT 06705 800-874-0029
GRE	Great Plains National (Children's Television Workshop) P.O. Box 80669 Lincoln, NE 68501-0669 800-228-4630
HPK	H.P. Kopplemann, Inc. 140 Van Block Avenue Hartford, CT 06141-0145 800-243-7724
HAL	HAL Leonard 7777 W. Bluemound Road P.O. Box 13819 Milwaukee, WI 53213 414-774-3630
HAM	Hammond Incorporated 515 Valley Street Maplewood, NJ 07040 800-526-4953
HAR	Harcourt Brace School Publishers 6277 Sea Harbor Drive Orlando, FL 32887 800-225-5425
HAW	Hawkhill Associates, Inc. 125 E. Gilman Street P.O. Box 1029 Madison, WI 53701-1029 800-422-4295

HEA   Health Education Services
               10200 Jefferson Boulevard
               Room H31
               P.O. Box 802
               Culver City, CA 90232-0802
               800-421-4246

HEAT   D.C. Heath and Company
               125 Spring Street
               Lexington, MA 02173
               800-334-3284

HIG   High/Scope Press
               600 N. River Street
               Ypsilanti, MI 48198-2898
               800-40-PRESS

HOL   Holt, Rinehart and Winston
               6277 Sea Harbor Drive
               Orlando, FL 32821-9816
               800-225-5425
               (same as Harcourt Brace)

HOT   Hotho & Co.
               Dept. H89
               P.O. Box 9738
               Fort Worth, TX 76147-2738
               817-335-1833

HOU   Houghton Mifflin
               222 Berkeley Street
               Boston, MA 02116-3764
               800-733-2828

HRM   HRM Video
               175 Tompkins Avenue
               Pleasantville, NY 10570-9973
               800-431-2050

HUB   Hubbard Scientific
               P.O. Box 760C
               Chippewa Falls, WI 54729-0760
               800-323-8368

HUM

Humanities Software, Inc.
408 Columbia Street
Suite 222
P.O. Box 950
Hood River, OR 97031
541-386-6737

IDE

Ideal School Supply Company
11000 S. Lavergne Avenue
Oak Lawn, IL 60453
800-845-8149

INC

Incentive Publications, Inc.
3835 Cleghorn Avenue
Nashville, TN 37215-2532
800-421-2830

IND

Indian House
P.O. Box 472
Taos, NM 87571
505-776-2953

INS

Instructional Fair, Inc.
P.O. Box 1650
Grand Rapids, MI 49501
800-253-5469

INST

Instructional Video, Inc.
727 'O' Street
Lincoln, NE 68508-1323
800-228-0164

JWES

J. Weston Walch, Publisher
321 Valley Street
P.O. Box 658
Portland, ME 04104-0658
800-341-6094

JAB

Jabberwocky
P.O. Box H
Novato, CA 94948
800-227-2020

JAC　　　　　　　　Jackdaws Publications
　　　　　　　　　　Division of Golden Owl Publishing
　　　　　　　　　　P.O. Box 503
　　　　　　　　　　Amawalk, NY 10501
　　　　　　　　　　914-962-6911

JAN　　　　　　　　January Productions
　　　　　　　　　　210 Sixth Avenue
　　　　　　　　　　P.O. Box 66
　　　　　　　　　　Hawthorne, NJ 07507-0066
　　　　　　　　　　800-451-7450

JOS　　　　　　　　Jostens Learning
　　　　　　　　　　9920 Pacific Heights Boulevard, Suite 500
　　　　　　　　　　San Diego, CA 92121
　　　　　　　　　　800-422-4339

JUD　　　　　　　　Judy/Instructo
　　　　　　　　　　4350 Equity Drive
　　　　　　　　　　P.O. Box 2649
　　　　　　　　　　Columbus, OH 43216
　　　　　　　　　　800-321-3106

KID　　　　　　　　Kidsrights
　　　　　　　　　　10100 Park Cedar Drive
　　　　　　　　　　Charlotte, NC 28210
　　　　　　　　　　800-892-KIDS

KIM　　　　　　　　Kimbo Educational
　　　　　　　　　　Dept. X
　　　　　　　　　　P.O. Box 477
　　　　　　　　　　Long Branch, NJ 07740-0477
　　　　　　　　　　800-631-2187

KNO　　　　　　　　Knowledge Unlimited
　　　　　　　　　　P.O. Box 52
　　　　　　　　　　Madison, WI 53707-0052
　　　　　　　　　　800-356-2303

LAU　　　　　　　　Laureate Learning Systems Inc.
　　　　　　　　　　110 East Spring Street
　　　　　　　　　　Winooski, VT 05404-1898
　　　　　　　　　　800-562-6801

LEA   The Learning Seed
                  330 Telser Road
                  Lake Zurich, IL 60047
                  800-634-4941

LEG   Lego Dacta
                  555 Taylor Road
                  P.O. Box 1600
                  Enfield, CT 06083-1600
                  800-527-8339

LIB   Library Video Company
                  P.O. Box 1110
                  Bala Cynwyd, PA 19004
                  800-843-3620

MAC   Macmillan/McGraw-Hill
                  220 East Danieldale Road
                  De Soto, TX 75115
                  800-442-9685

MAH   Maher
                  P.O. Box 420
                  Littleton, CO 80160
                  303-798-6830

ML   McDougal Littell
                  P.O. Box 1667
                  Evanston, IL 60204
                  800-323-5435

MEC   MECC
                  3490 Lexington Avenue North
                  St. Paul, MN 55126
                  612-481-3500
                  800-228-3504

MEDB   Media Basics Video
                  Lighthouse Square
                  705 Boston Post Road
                  Guilford, CT 06437
                  203-458-2505

MEDM   Media Materials
                111 Kane Street
                Baltimore, MD 21224

MIL   Milliken Publishing Company
                1100 Research Boulevard
                P.O. Box 21579
                St. Louis, MO 63132
                800-325-4136

MILT   Milton Bradley Company
                443 Shaker Road
                East Longmeadow, MA 01028
                413-525-6411

MIN   Mindplay
                P.O. Box 36491
                Tucson, AZ 85740
                800-221-7911

MODC   Modern Curriculum Press
                4350 Equity Drive
                P.O. Box 2649
                Columbus, OH 43216
                800-321-3106

MODT   Modern Talking Picture Service, Inc.
                5000 Park Street N
                St. Petersburg, FL 33709-9977
                800-243-6877

MOV   Movies Unlimited
                6736 Castor Avenue
                Philadelphia, PA 19149-2184
                800-523-0823

NAN   Nancy Renfro
                P.O. Box 164226
                Austin, TX 78716
                800-933-5512

NAS   NASCO
                901 Janesville Avenue
                P.O. Box 901
                Fort Atkinson, WI 53538-0901
                800-558-9595

NAEYC   National Association for the Education of Young
                 Children
               1509 16th Street, NW
               Washington, DC 20036-1426
               800-424-2460

NCTE   National Council of Teachers of English
               1111 W. Kenyon Road
               Urbana, IL 61801-1096
               800-369-6283

NCTM   National Council of Teachers of Mathematics
               1906 Association Drive
               Reston, VA 22091-1593
               800-235-7566

NATG   National Geographic Society
               Educational Services
               P.O. Box 98019
               Washington, DC 20090-8019
               800-368-2728

NATS   National School Products
               101 East Broadway
               Maryville, TN 37801-2498
               800-627-9393

NSTA   National Science Teachers Association
               1840 Wilson Boulevard
               Arlington, VA 22201-3000
               800-722-NSTA

NEW   New York Times
               NYT Educational Media
               105 Terry Drive
               Suite 120
               Newtown, PA 18940-3425
               800-991-1112

NOV   Novel Units
               P.O. Box 1461
               Palatine, IL 60078
               708-253-8200

NYS   Nystrom
               3333 Elston Avenue
               Chicago, IL 60618-5898
               800-621-8086

ONE   One Way Street
               P.O. Box 5077
               Englewood, CO 80155
               800-569-4537

OPT   Optical Data School Media
               30 Technology Drive
               Warren, NJ 07059
               800-524-2481

ORA   Orange Cherry New Media Schoolhouse
               P.O. Box 390
               69 Westchester Avenue
               Pound Ridge, NY 10576
               800-672-6002

PBS   PBS Video
               1320 Braddock Place
               Alexandria, VA 22314
               800-344-3337

PEG   Pegasus Learning Company
               18 E. Monument Avenue
               Colorado Springs, CO 80903
               800-713-2165

PER   Perfection Learning Corporation
               1000 North Second Avenue
               Logan, IA 51546-1099
               800-831-4190

PIE   Pied Piper
               9710 DeSoto Avenue
               Chatsworth, CA 91311-4409
               800-367-2467

POS   Poster Education
               Box 8774
               Asheville, NC 28814
               800-858-0969

PRE   Prentice-Hall
           School Division of Simon & Schuster
           4350 Equity Drive
           P.O. Box 2649
           Columbus, OH 43272-4480
           800-848-9500

PUP   Puppet Productions
           P.O. Box 1066
           DeSoto, TX 75123-1066
           800-854-9151

QUE   Queue, Inc.
           338 Commerce Drive
           Fairfield, CT 06430
           800-232-2224

RAI   Rainbow Educational Media
           3043 Barrow Drive
           Raleigh, NC 27604
           800-331-4047

ROL   Roland Collection
           22-D Hollywood Avenue
           Ho-Ho-Kus, NJ 07423
           800-597-6526

S&S   S & S Arts & Crafts
           P.O. Box 513
           Colchester, CT 06415-0513
           800-243-9232

SAR   Sargent-Welch
           911 Commerce Court
           Buffalo Grove, IL 60089-2375
           800-727-4368

SCH   Scholastic, Inc.
           2931 East McCarty Street
           Jefferson City, MO 65101
           573-636-5271

SCI   Science Kit & Boreal Laboratories
           777 East Park Drive
           Tonawanda, NY 14150-6784
           800-828-7777

SCOF   Scott Foresman
            1900 East Lake Avenue
            Glenview, IL 60025
            800-554-4411

SCOR   Scott Resources
            P.O. Box 2121D
            Fort Collins, CO 80522
            303-484-7445

SIG   Signals
            WGBH Educational Foundation
            P.O. Box 64428
            St. Paul, MN 55164-0428
            800-669-9696

SIL   Silver Burdett Ginn
            4350 Equity Drive
            P.O. Box 2649
            Columbus, OH 43216
            614-876-0371

SIM   Simulation Training Systems
            Box 910
            Del Mar, CA 92014
            800-942-2900

SOC   Social Studies School Service
            10200 Jefferson Boulevard
            Room B31
            P.O. Box 802
            Culver City, CA 90232-0802
            800-421-4246

SOCIET   Society for Visual Education, Inc.
            6677 North Northwest Highway
            Chicago, IL 60631-1304
            800-829-1900

SOF   Software Express, Inc.
            4128-A South Boulevard
            Charlotte, NC 28209
            800-527-7638

SPO   Spoken Arts
801 94th Avenue North
St. Petersburg, FL 33702
800-326-4090

SRA   SRA/McGraw-Hill
P.O. Box 543
Blacklick, OH 43004-0543
800-843-8855

STE   Steck-Vaughn Company
P.O. Box 26015
Austin, TX 78755
800-531-5015

SUM   Summit Learning
P.O. Box 493
Ft. Collins, CO 80522
800-500-8817

SUNB   Sunburst Communications
39 Washington Avenue
Pleasantville, NY 10570-0040
800-431-1934

SUND   Sundance Publishing
234 Taylor Street
P.O. Box 1326
Littleton, MA 01460-9936
800-343-8204

TEACHE   Teacher Support Software, Inc.
1035 N.W. 57th Street
Gainesville, FL 32605-4486
800-524-6446

TEACHL   Teachers' Laboratory
24 Birge Street
P.O. Box 6480
Brattleboro, VT 05302
800-254-3457

THE   Therapy Skill Builders
555 Academic Court
San Antonio, TX 78204-2498
800-866-4446

TIG   Tiger Software
               One Datran Center
               Suite 1500
               9100 S. Dadeland Boulevard
               Miami, FL 33156
               800-238-4437

TIM   Time Life Education
               P.O. Box 85026
               Richmond, VA 23285-5026
               800-449-2010

TOM   Tom Snyder Productions, Inc.
               80 Coolidge Hill Road
               Watertown, MA 02172-2817
               800-342-0236

TRE   Trend Enterprises, Inc.
               c/o Edumate Educational Materials, Inc.
               2231 Morena Boulevard
               San Diego, CA 92110
               619-275-7117

TVO   TVOntario
               143 West Franklin Street
               Suite 206
               Chapel Hill, NC 27516
               800-331-9566

UNI   United Transparency, Inc.
               435 Main Street
               Johnson City, NY 13790
               607-729-6368

VID   Videodiscovery, Inc.
               1700 Westlake Ave. N.
               Suite 600
               Seattle, WA 98109-3012
               800-548-3472

VIS   Vis-Ed
               Visual Education Association
               581 West Leffel Lane
               P.O. Box 1666
               Springfield, OH 45501
               800-243-7070

WAR   Ward's
        P.O. Box 92912
        Rochester, NY 14692-9012
        800-962-2660

WAT   Watten Poe Teaching Resource Center
        P.O. Box 1509
        San Leandro, CA 94577
        800-833-3389

WES   Weston Woods
        Weston, CT 06883-1199
        800-243-5020

WFF   WFF'N PROOF Learning Games
        1490 South Boulevard
        Ann Arbor, MI 48104
        313-665-2269

WRI   The Writing Company
        10200 Jefferson Boulevard
        Room WR2
        P.O. Box 802
        Culver City, CA 90232-0802
        800-421-4246

ZAN   Zaner Bloser
        2200 West Fifth Avenue
        P.O. Box 16764
        Columbus, OH 43216-6764
        800-421-3018

ZEN   Zenger Media
        10200 Jefferson Boulevard
        Room 91
        P.O. Box 802
        Culver City, CA 90232-0802
        800-421-4246

ZTE   Ztek Co.
        P.O. Box 11768
        Lexington, KY 40577-1768
        800-247-1603

Chapter Eighteen

Curriculum Guides, Frameworks, and Standards on the Web

State Departments of Education Sites

California

http://www.Worldtouch.com/Framework/Framework.html
Provides descriptions of frameworks for various curriculum areas.
http://goldmine.cde.ca.gov/
Provides link to gopher which gives list of adopted textbooks only;
no curriculum guides.

Colorado

http://www.cde.state.co.us/ftpcde.htm#standards
Provides access to curriculum standards for various curriculum
areas.

Delaware

gopher://gopher.ed.gov:1000/11/initiatives/stan-doc/stan
Provides access to various curriculum standards.

Kentucky

http://www.kde.state.ky.us/caa/curric.html
Provides access to curriculum frameworks (nicely interfaced).

Massachusetts

http://info.doe.Mass.edu/doedocs/frameworks
Provides access to curriculum frameworks.

Michigan

http://www.mde.state.mi.us/off/index.html
Provides access to gopher for curriculum guides.
gopher://gopher.mde.state.mi.us/11/serv/curric/corecur
Provides direct access to gopher.

Missouri

http://services.dese.state.mo.us/standards/
Provides access to curriculum standards for most subject areas.

Nebraska

http://www.nde.state.ne.us/ss/ss.html
Provides access to *K–12 Social Studies Framework* with links to lesson
plans related to the theme, as well as other links with related content
and resources.

New Hampshire

http://www.state.nh.us/doe/math.htm
Provides mathematics curriculum framework.

New Jersey

http://prism.prs.k12.nj.us/www/011/NJccc.html
Provides core curriculum content standards.

New York

http://www.nysed.gov/
Provides link to gopher for access to curriculum guides.
gopher://unix10.nysed.gov:70/11/emsc
Provides direct access to above gopher.
http://www.mac.cnyric.org/frameworks/hperhe/curriculum/
Provides access to health and physical education framework.

North Carolina

http://www.dpi.state.nc.us/curriculum/crrclmMtrx.html
Provides access to the state's standard course of study for
various grades and curriculum subjects.

Ohio

http://www.ode.Ohio.gov/
Provides access to gopher for *Prekindergarten–Grade 12 Standards for Ohio Schools.*

South Carolina

http://scdoe.usconnect.com/framewks/foreign.htm
Provides foreign language framework.

Utah

http://www.usoe.k12.ut.us/
Provides link to gopher for curriculum guides.

Wisconsin

http://www.State.Wi.us/agencies/dpi
Provides access to curriculum publications catalog.

Other Sites

K–12 Curriculum Resources on the Web

http://www.lloyd.com/k12curriculum.html
Provides links to K–12 curriculum resources on the Web including frameworks and curriculum projects.

Standards for K–12 Education

http://www.mcrel.org/standards-benchmarks/
Provides nationally developed standards for all major disciplines, grades primary through senior high school. Contains an excellent search capability to locate standards and supporting items which relate to searched concepts and terms.

K–12 Sources, Curriculum, Lesson Plans

http://www.execpc.com/~dboals/k-12.html
Provides an extensive listing of sites dealing with education; many curriculum projects are included.

Developing Educational Standards

http://putwest.boces.org/standards.html
Provides a comprehensive listing of sites where curriculum
standards for most K–12 curriculum areas can be found online or
information about the standards can be found. The standards
documents have been prepared by various states and professional
organizations.

Artsedge Curriculum Connection

http://artsedge.kennedy-center.org/artsedge.html
Provides access to curriculum standards and frameworks for the
arts.

NCTE

http://www.ncte.org/
Provides online access to the catalog of publications of the National
Council of Teachers of English as well as Internet resources for
English teachers, i.e., WWW sites, listservs, and gopher servers.

NCTM Curriculum and Evaluation

http://www.enc.org/online/NCTM/280dtoc1.html
Provides access to *Standards for School Mathematics* from the National
Council of Teachers of Mathematics.

Mathematics Archives: K–12 Teaching Materials

http://archives.math.utk.edu/k12.html
Provides a very comprehensive listing of links to mathematics
curriculum materials and projects.

Steve's Dump

http://forum.swarthmore.edu/~steve/
Provides a comprehensive listing of links to all kinds of
mathematics curriculum resources on the Internet; contains a search
feature.

Pathways to School Improvement

http://www.ncrel.org/ncrel/sdrs/pathwayg.htm
Explains the new science and math standards and provides links
for the development of understandings of their applications.

State Curriculum Frameworks

http://www.enc.org:80/frame.htm
Provides curriculum frameworks particularly for mathematics and science; many states can be accessed at this site.

Curriculum Support Materials

http://www.enc.org:80/curriculum.htm
Provides various curriculum documents pertaining to curriculum standards and implementation for mathematics and science.

Eisenhower National Clearinghouse

http://www.enc.org/
Provides a wealth of information about mathematics and science curriculum including documents, lessons, frameworks, and a resource finder that allows searches for curriculum materials.

National Science Education Standards

http://www.nap.edu/nap/online/nses/
Provides access to the nationally developed science standards.

National Science Teachers Association

http://www.nsta.org/
Provides information about NSTA publications, projects, and on-line resources.

Pluto Express Curriculum Guides for Educators (NASA)

http://www.jpl.nasa.gov/pluto/cg-top.htm
Provides curriculum guides and activities on space travel which can be used with a free videotape. These curriculum guides have been designed to provide the teacher at any grade level with materials that involve students actively as well as imaginatively.

Birds: Our Environmental Indicators

http://www.nceet.snre.umich.edu/curriculum/toc.html
Provides curriculum guides from Earth Generation's *New York Educator's Guide* for junior high school students investigating environmental issues relevant to the Great Lakes.

American History Archive Project

http://www.ilt.columbia.edu/k12.history.aha.html
Provides curriculum for middle and secondary school students and
teachers dealing with the Revolutionary War and the Civil War,
including video and audio clips.

National Standards for Grades K–4 History

http:www.sscnet.ucla.edu/nchs/usk4-toc.htm
Provides online version of the paper edition published by the
National Center for History in the Schools.

National Standards for United States History

http://www.sscnet.ucla.edu/nchs/us-toc.htm
Provides online version of the paper edition published by the
National Center for History in the Schools.

NCSS

http://www.ncss.org/online/
Provides the text of the National Council for the Social Studies
document *Expect Excellence: Curriculum Standards for Social Studies.*
Also provides online access to NCSS publications which includes a
list of other social studies standards published by NCSS or other
agencies.

National Standards for Physical Education

http://www.aahperd.org/naspe/stdspe.html
Provides list of nationally developed content standards for physical
education with sample objectives and benchmarks for grades four
and eight.

ERIC Clearinghouses

Each of the following sites provides various curriculum digests
and publications by the discipline emphasis of the particular
clearinghouse:

Reading, English, and Communication

http://www.indiana.edu/~eric_rec/

Social Studies/Science Education

http://www.indiana.edu/~ssdc/eric-chess.html

Elementary and Early Childhood Education

gopher://ericps.ed.uiuc.edu/

Science, Mathematics, and Environmental Education

http://www.ericse.ohio-state.edu/eric/maths.html

Chapter Nineteen

Textbook Publisher Sites on the Web

The following are the Web addresses for the textbook publishers that have home pages on the World Wide Web. Each one tells something about its publications. Houghton Mifflin has gone further by providing links to various education sites.

Addison Wesley	http://www.aw.com/awpc.html
Houghton Mifflin	http://www.hmco.com/hmco/ school/school.html
Key Curriculum Press	http://www.keypress.com/
McDougal Littell	http://www.hmco.com/hmco /mcdougal/McDougal.html
Rigby	http://www.reedbooks.com.au/ rigby/
Scholastic	http://www.scholastic.com/
South-Western	http://itp.thomson.com:2345/ swpco.html
The Wright Group	http://www.wrightgroup.com/twg/

Chapter Twenty

Internet Teaching Activities Sources

Lesson Plans and Teaching Strategies for Social Studies

http://www.csun.edu/~hcedu013/plans.html
Provides links to hundreds of lesson plans and teaching activities
for all ages and social studies topics; many linked to gopher sites.

Teaching Current Events Through Newspapers and TV

http://www.csun.edu/~hcedu013/cevents.html
Provides links to various lesson plans using the newspaper and TV.

MegaMath

http://www.c3.lanl.gov/mega-math/
From the Computer Research and Applications Group at Los
Alamos National Laboratory, this site provides many creative
teaching ideas in math.

Appetizers and Lessons for Math & Reason

http://www.cam.org/~aselby/lesson.html
Provides various exercises to help students understand algebra and
proofs.

Weather Unit

http://faldo.atmos.uiuc.edu/WEATHER/weather.html
For students in the elementary grades; lessons integrate math,
science, geography, and language arts as the subject of weather is
studied.

Busy Teachers' Website

http://www.gatech.edu/lcc/idt/students/cole/proj/K–12/
  TOC.h tml
Provides links to lesson plans and teaching activities in a variety of curriculum areas as well as curriculum content information.

AIMS Education Foundation

http://204.161.33.100/
Provides various math teaching activities, especially integrating math and science.

Eisenhower National Clearinghouse (ENC)

http://www.enc.org/
Provides links primarily to math and science lessons, but has a nice activity search feature for all major curriculum areas and K–8 grade levels.

AskERIC Lesson Plans

Gopher://ericir.syr.edu.70/11/Lesson
Lesson plans are provided for a variety of K–12 curriculum areas; has a search function using keywords.

Beakman and Jax Science Stuff

http://www.nbn.com/YOUCAN/
Some interesting science activities are presented.

Kathy Schrock's Guide for Educators

http://www.capecod.net/schrockguide/
Provides extensive resources for K–12 students and teachers covering 20 major categories of curriculum subject matter; excellent source of background material and curriculum content as well as teaching activities.

Steve's Dump

http://forum.Swarthmore.edu/~steve/
Provides a comprehensive listing of links to all kinds of math teaching activities and lessons as well as math content material on the Internet; also has a search feature.

Children's Literature—Resources for Teachers

http://www.ucalgary.ca/~dkbrown/rteacher.html
Provides links to all kinds of resources related to children's
literature and young adult literature including lesson plans.

Ron Mackinnon's Teacher Resources

http://juliet.stfx.ca/people/stu/X94emj/teacher.htm
Provides a comprehensive list of K–12 curriculum resource sites
including lesson plans and teaching activities.

K–12 Sources, Curriculum, Lesson Plans

http://www.execpc.com/~dboals/K–12.html
An extensive listing of sites is provided that deal with K–12
curriculum; many provide teaching activity ideas.

Teacher Topics

http://www.asd.k12.ak.us/Andrews/Teacher Topics.html
Although this site does not provide teaching activities, it is worth
mentioning because it provides typical unit curriculum topics
taught in the elementary school and then provides links to
curriculum subject matter to support each topic.

Classroom Resources—Activities

http://www.nceet.snre.umich.edu/activities.html
Lesson plans are provided in the areas of energy, ecology, and
conservation.

School Activities—Contents

http://www.ag.uiuc.edu/~disaster/csndactx.html
Provides activities to use with K–12 students dealing with natural
disasters.

SETI Institute Education Programs

http://www.seti-inst.edu/ed-top.html
Sample lesson plans are provided for the published supplementary
science curriculum for elementary and middle grades Life in the
Universe Curriculum Project.

Lesson Plans: Maps—What Do Maps Show?

http://www.usgs.gov/education/teacher/what-do-maps-show/
   index.html
Produced by U.S. Geological Survey, map skill lessons are provided
for upper elementary and junior high school level.

Ocean Environment Classroom Activities

http://www.bev.net/education/seaworld/teacherguides.html
Provides lesson plans for various grade levels, K–12, concerning the
ocean environment that integrate science, math, geography, art, and
language.

Solid Waste Classroom Activities

gopher://nceet.snre.umich.edu:777/11/activities/cornell
Lesson plans are provided for elementary and secondary grades
involving environment and conservation.

Collaborative Lesson Archive

http://faldo.atmos.uiuc.edu/TUA_Home.html
Various K–12 lesson plans primarily on science topics are provided
with links to curriculum content in other fields.

Big Sky

gopher://bvsd.k12.co.us/11/Educational_Resources/Lesson_P
   lans/Big%20SKY/Science
Provides lesson plans for many different curriculum areas for
grades K–12.

Scholastic Internet Center

http://www.scholastic.com/public/Learning Libraries.html
Presents detailed lesson plans in middle school science. Also, there
are lesson plans for language arts and literature, technology, and
the seasons.

Mathematics Lesson Plans

http://www.cs.rice.edu/~sboone/Lessons/lptitle.html
Various math teaching activities are presented utilizing the Internet.

Teacher-Developed Lesson Plans

http://www.cea.berkeley.edu/Education/teacher-developed.html
Contains earth and space science lesson plans for middle, junior
high, and high school students.

Lesson Plans, Cedar Lane Center

http://www.usgs.gov/cedar/lesson.html
Provides links to many lesson plans in language arts, math, science,
and social studies; very extensive compilation.

Teacher Talk Forum

http://education.indiana.edu/cas/ttforum/lesson.html
Provides detailed lessons collected from teachers from various areas
of the United States. These lessons are primarily on the secondary
level in the curriculum areas of art, computers, foreign language,
health and safety, home economics, language arts, music, physical
education, reading, science, social studies, and special education.

Lesson Plans On-line

http:www.sdserv.org/tie/lessons.html
Provides links to various lesson plan sites dealing with various
curriculum areas.

SAMI—Lesson Plans and Projects

http://www.c3.lanl.gov/~jspeck/lessons.shtml
Provides links to various lesson plans and curriculum project sites.

Secondary School English Lesson Plan Index

http://www.aladdin.co.uk/sihe/citygate/lessonplans/index.html
Provides lesson plans for Shakespeare and poetry.

Lesson Plans

http://curry.edschool.virginia.edu/~kpj5e/whales/LessonPl
ans.html
Elementary level lesson plans on whales are presented.

Air Quality Lesson Plans and Data

http://www.tnrcc.state.tx.us/air/lesson_plans.html
Presents lesson plans on air pollution for elementary grades.

Science and Math on the Internet

http://alcom.kent.edu/ALCOM/k12/Lesson_Plans.html
Created by teams of teachers of science, math, and technology, and
librarians; provides science and math lesson plans for elementary
and secondary levels.

CNN Lesson Plans

gopher://ericir.syr.edu/11/Lesson/CNN
Presents daily lesson plans for CNN Newsroom Daily.

Galileo

http://www-hpcc.astro.washington.edu/scied/galileo.html
Provides science lesson plans mostly on the K–6 level.

Lesson Plan URLs

http://tfcserv.edu.yorku.ca/~tcs/~rfouchaux/les_plan.htm
Provides access to multiple links for lesson plans for various
curriculum subjects and levels.

Lesson Plans and Activities

http://www.mcrel.org/connect/lesson.html
Provides extensive links to lesson plans for elementary and
secondary grades in the areas of math, science, language arts, ESL,
and social studies.

Creative Lesson Plans in Art

http://www.bway.net/~starlite/projects.htm
Art lesson plans for K–6 are provided.

Genetics

http://www.kumc.edu/GEC/lessons.html
Presents lesson plans on genetics for secondary grades.

Lesson Plans—Elementary

http://www.wa.gov/courts/educate/lessons/lpelem.htm
Various law-related lesson plans are provided for elementary and
junior high school levels.

FIRNS's Best Lesson Plans

http://ouray.cudenver.edu/~lcsherry/firnstuff/index.html
Telecommunication-based lesson plans are presented for grades
K–12 and cover a variety of curriculum areas.

Art Lesson Plans

http://curry.edschool.virginia.edu/curry/class/Museums/
   Teac her_Guide/Art
Provides art lesson plans for elementary and secondary levels.

Center for Civic Education Lesson Plans

http://www.primenet.com/~cce/lesson_plans.html
Lessons are presented for elementary and secondary school
students in the area of civics.

Wally's Web

http://accucomm1.accucomm.america.net/~hpowers/wally.html
Provides a very comprehensive listing of links to lesson plans in all
curriculum areas and levels.

Project Athena

http://www.athena.ivv.nasa.gov/index.html
Provides science curriculum lesson plans relating to oceans, the
atmosphere, earth science, and space/astronomy.

Chapter Twenty-one

Teaching Activities on the Internet by Curriculum Area

The following listings are designed to save the curriculum librarian time in working with users who are interested in finding teaching activities and lesson plans on the Internet that pertain to a particular curriculum discipline. Each of the sites in chapter 20 that has activities for more than one curriculum area was analyzed and each curriculum area covered was noted so that it could be grouped in this chapter with other sites having activities for that discipline. Also, those sites that pertain to just one discipline were also found and placed in that discipline's list below. Chapter 22 lists sites that provide curriculum content links for the various disciplines that would be useful in supporting lesson plans. (All URLs are K–12 unless designated.)

Art Teaching Activities

AskERIC Lesson Plans

gopher://ericir.syr.edu:70/11/Lesson

Kathy Schrock's Guide for Educators

http://www.capecod.net/schrockguide/

Big Sky

gopher://bvsd.k12.co.us/11/Educational_Resources/Le
    sson_Plans/Big Sky

Creative Lesson Plans in Art

http://www.bway.net/~starlite/projects.htm

Art Lesson Plans

http://curry.edschool.virginia.edu/curry/class/museums/
Teacher_Gu ide/Art

Foreign Language Teaching Activities

AskERIC Lesson Plans

gopher://ericir.syr.edu:70/11/Lesson

Language Arts Teaching Activities

Weather Unit (elementary)

http://faldo.atmos.uiuc.edu/WEATHER/weather.html

AskERIC Lesson Plans

gopher://ericir.syr.edu:70/11/Lesson

Children's Literature—Resources for Teachers

http://www.ucalgary.ca/~dkbrown/rteacher.html

Kathy Schrock's Guide for Educators

http://www.capecod.net/schrockguide/

Ron Mackinnon's Teacher Resources

http://juliet.stfx.ca/people/stu/x94emj/teacher.htm

K–12 Sources, Curriculum, Lesson Plans

http://www.execpc.com/~dboals/k-12.html

Big Sky

gopher://bvsd.k12.co.US:70/11/

Scholastic Internet Center

http://www.Scholastic.com/public/Learning Libraries.html

Lesson Plans, Cedar Lane Center

http://www.usgs.gov/cedar/lesson.html

Teacher Talk Forum (primarily secondary)

http://education.indiana.edu/cas/ttforum/lesson.html

Lesson Plans On-Line

http://www.sdserv.org/tie/lessons.html

Secondary School English Lesson Plan Index

http://www.aladdin.co.uk/sihe/citygate/lessonplans/index
.htm

Lesson Plan URLs

http://tfcserv.edu.yorku.ca/~tcs/~rfouchaux/les_plan.htm

Lesson Plans and Activities

http://www.mcrel.org/connect/lesson.html

Mathematics Teaching Activities

Mathematics Archives: K–12 Teaching Materials

http://archives.math.utk.edu/k12.html

MegaMath

http://www.c3.lanl.gov/mega-math/

Appetizers and Lessons for Math & Reason (secondary)

http://www.cam.org/~aselby/lesson.html

AIMS Education Foundation

http://204.161.33.100/

Eisenhower National Clearinghouse (ENC)

http://www.enc.org/

AskERIC Lesson Plans

gopher://ericir.syr.edu:70/11/Lesson

Kathy Schrock's Guide for Educators

http://www.capecod.net/schrockguide/

Steve's Dump

http://forum.swarthmore.edu/~steve/

Ron Mackinnon's Teacher Resources

http://juliet.stfx.ca/people/stu/x94emj/teacher.htm

K–12 Sources, Curriculum, Lesson Plans

http://www.execpc.com/~dboals/k-12.html

Mathematics Lesson Plans

http://www.cs.rice.edu/~sboone/Lessons/lptitle.html

Lesson Plans, Cedar Lane Center

http://www.usgs.gov/cedar/lesson.html

Lesson Plans On-Line

http://www.sdserv.org/tie/lessons.html

SAMI—Lesson Plans and Projects

http://www.c3.lanl.gov/~jspeck/lessons.shtml

Science and Math on the Internet—Lesson Plans

http://alcom.kent.edu/ALCOM/K12/Lesson_Plans.html

Lesson Plan URLs

http://tfcserv.edu.yorku.ca/~tcs/~rfouchaux/les_plan.htm

Lesson Plans and Activities

http://www.mcrel.org/connect/lesson.html

Music Teaching Activities

Teacher Talk Forum

http://education.Indiana.edu/cas/ttforum.html

AskERIC Lesson Plans

gopher://ericir.syr.edu:70/11/Lesson

Ron MacKinnon's Educational Bookmarks

http://juliet.stfx.ca/people/stu/x94emj/bookmark.html

Music Educators' Lesson Plans Resources

http://www.gnatnet.net/~jjbrenan/database.html

K–12 Resources for Music Educators

http://www.isd77.k12.mn.us/resources/staffpages/shirk/
cindys.page.k12.lin k.html

Science Teaching Activities

Weather Unit (elementary)

http://faldo.atmos.uiuc.edu/WEATHER/weather.html

AIMS Education Foundation

http://204.161.33.100/

Eisenhower National Clearinghouse (ENC)

http://www.enc.org/

AskERIC Lesson Plans

gopher://ericir.syr.edu:70/11/Lesson

Beakman and Jax Science Stuff

http://www.nbn.com/youcan/

Kathy Schrock's Guide for Educators

http://www.capecod.net/schrockguide/

Ron Mackinnon's Teacher Resources

http://juliet.stfx.ca/people/stu/x94emj/teacher.htm

K–12 Sources, Curriculum, Lesson Plans

http://www.execpc.com/~dboals/k-12.html

Classroom Resources—Activities

http://www.nceet.snre.umich.edu/

School Activities—Contents

http://www.ag.uiuc.edu/~disaster/csndactx.html

SETI Institute Education Programs

http://www.seti-inst.edu/ed—top.html

Ocean Environment Classroom Activities

http://www.bev.net/education/seaworld/teacherguides.html

Solid Waste Classroom Activities

gopher://nceet.snre.umich.edu:777/11/activities/cornell

Collaborative Lesson Archive

http://faldo.atmos.uiuc.edu/TUA_Home.html

Big Sky

gopher://bvsd.k12.co.US:70/11/

Scholastic Internet Center

http://www.Scholastic.com/public/Learning Libraries.html

Teacher-Developed Lesson Plans (middle school—senior high)

http://www.cea.berkeley.edu/Education/teacher-developed.html

Lesson Plans, Cedar Lane Center

http://www.usgs.gov/cedar/lesson.html

Teacher Talk Forum

http://education.indiana.edu/cas/ttforum/lesson.html

Lesson Plans On-Line

http://www.sdserv.org/tie/lessons.html

SAMI—Lesson Plans and Projects

http://www.c3.lanl.gov/~jspeck/lessons.shtml

Lesson Plans (elementary level plans on whales)

http://curry.edschool.virginia.edu/~kpj5e/whales/LessonPlans.html

Air Quality Lesson Plans and Data (elementary)

http://www.tnrcc.state.tx.us/air/lesson-plans.html

Science and Math on the Internet—Lesson Plans

http://alcom.kent.edu/ALCOM/K12/Lesson_Plans.html

Galileo (K–6)

http://www-hpcc.astro.washington.edu/scied/galileo.html

Lesson Plan URLs

http://tfcserv.edu.yorku.ca/~tcs/~rfouchaux/les_plan.htm

Lesson Plans and Activities

http://www.mcrel.org/connect/lesson.html

Genetics (secondary)

http://www.kumc.edu/GEC/lessons.html

FIRNS's Best Lesson Plans

http://ouray.cudenver.edu/~lcsherry/firnstuff/index.html

Project Athena

http://www.athena.ivv.nasa.gov/index.html

Social Studies Teaching Activities

Lesson Plans and Teaching Strategies for Social Studies

http://www.csun.edu/~hcedu013/plans.html

Teaching Current Events Through Newspapers and TV

http://www.csun.edu/~hcedu013/cevents.html

Kathy Schrock's Guide for Educators

http://www.capecod.net/schrockguide/

Weather Unit (elementary)

http://faldo.atmos.uiuc.edu/WEATHER/weather.html

AskERIC Lesson Plans

gopher://ericir.syr.edu:70/11/Lesson

Ron Mackinnon's Teacher Resources

http://juliet.stfx.ca/people/stu/x94emj/teacher.htm

K–12 Sources, Curriculum, Lesson Plans

http://www.execpc.com/~dboals/k-12.html

Lesson Plans: Maps—What Do Maps Show? (upper elementary and junior high)
http://www.usgs.gov/education/teacher/what-do-maps-show/index.html

Big Sky

gopher://bvsd.k12.co.US:70/11/

Lesson Plans, Cedar Lane Center

http://www.usgs.gov/cedar/lesson.html

Teacher Talk Forum (primarily secondary)

http://education.indiana.edu/cas/ttforum/lesson.html

Lesson Plans On-Line

http://www.sdserv.org/tie/lessons.html

SAMI—Lesson Plans and Projects

http://www.c3.lanl.gov/~jspeck/lessons.shtml

CNN Lesson Plans

gopher://ericir.syr.edu/11/Lesson/CNN

Lesson Plan URLs

http://tfcserv.edu.yorku.ca/~tcs/~rfouchaux/les_plan.htm

Lesson Plans and Activities

http://www.mcrel.org/connect/lesson.html

Lesson Plans—Elementary (law-related lesson plans, elementary and junior high)
http://www.wa.gov/courts/educate/lessons/lpelem.htm

FIRNS's Best Lesson Plans

http://ouray.cudenver.edu/~lcsherry/firnstuff/index.html

Center for Civic Education Lesson Plans

http://www.primenet.com/~cce/lesson_plans.html

AskERIC Lesson Plans

gopher://ericir.syr.edu:70/11/Lesson

Chapter Twenty-two

Curriculum Content Resource Sites on the Internet

In addition to sites that describe teaching activities, there are numerous sites on the Internet that provide a plethora of curriculum resources to support lesson plans and activities. These consist of such items as documents, photographs, moving pictures, literature texts, charts, demonstrations, museums, etc., as well as much descriptive material to provide background for the subject matter being taught. Below are listed some sites that contain links to many of the sites that provide these important curriculum support materials.

Busy Teachers' Website K–12

http://www.gatech.edu/lcc/idt/Students/Cole/Proj/k-12/TOC.html

Kathy Schrock's Guide for Educators

http://www.capecod.net/schrockguide/

Ron Mackinnon's Teacher Resources

http://juliet.stfx.ca/people/stu/x94emj/teacher.htm

K–12 Sources, Curriculum, Lesson Plans

http://www.execpc.com/~dboals/k-12.html

Teacher Topics

http://www.asd.k12.ak.us/Andrews/Teacher Topics.html

Carrie's Sites for Educators
http://www.mtjeff.com/~bodenst/page5.html

K–12 Educational Resources
http://137.142.42.95/K-12/K-12 EducationalResources.html

K–12 Resources
http://www.informns.K12.mn.us/K12links.html

Education K–12
http://www.pointcom.com/gifs/reviews/edkt.htm

The World Wide Web Virtual Library: Education
http://www.csu.edu.au/education/library.html

History/Social Studies Web Site for K–12 Teachers
http://www.execpc.com/~dboals/boals.html

Social Science Resources
http://www.nde.state.ne.us/ss/ss.html

Yahoo: Education
http://www.yahoo.com/Education/

WebEd K–12 Curriculum Links
http://www.state.wi.us/agencies/dpi/www/WebEd.html

Eisenhower National Clearinghouse
http://www.enc.org/

Standards for K–12 Education
http://www.mcrel.org/standards-benchmarks/

Steve's Dump

http://forum.swarthmore.edu/~steve/

Mathematics Archives: K–12 Teaching Materials

http://archives.math.utk.edu/k12.html

Jan's Favorite K–12 Resources & Projects

http://www.state.wi.us/agencies/dpi/www/jans_bkm.html

K–12 Education Resources

http://www.ris.sdbor.edu/sdsd/k_12 EdRes.htm

Books On-line

http://-cgi.cs.cmu.edu/cgi-bin/book/maketitlepage

Amazing Picture Machine

http://www.ncrel.org/ncrtec/picture.htm

Pathways to School Improvement

http://www.ncrel.org/ncrel/sdrs/pathwayg.htm

K–12 Curriculum Resources on the Web

http://www.lloyd.com/k12curriculum.html

K–12 Curriculum Resources

http://www.ed.uiuc.edu/Education-add.html#K-12Curricul
um Resources

Beakman and Jax Science Stuff

http://www.nbn.com/youcan/

K–12 WWW Resources

http://www.leyada.jlm.k12.il/english/resources/

SAMI—Lesson Plans and Projects

http://www.c3.lanl.gov/~jspeck/lessons.shtml

Science, Math, and Other Educational Resources

http://-hpcc.astro.washington.edu/scied/science.html

American History Archive Project

http://www.ilt.columbia.edu/k12/history/aha.html

Library of Congress National Digital Library—American Memory

http://lcweb2.loc.gov/ammem/

Social Studies Sources

http://www.halcyon.com/howlevin/social studies.html

Social Studies and History Resources

http://www.halcyon.com/garycres/sshp/begin.html

Netspedition Amazon

http://sunsite.doc.ic.ac.uk/netspedition

MIMS (Midlands Improving Math and Science) Hub

http://scssi.scetv.org/mims

Chemistry Multimedia

http://www.ncl.ox.ac.uk/quicktime/index.html

Molecule of the Month

http://www.bris.ac.uk/Depts/Chemistry/MOTM/motm.htm

Weathernet

http://cirrus.sprl.umich.edu/wxnet/tropical.html

VolcanoWorld

http://volcano.und.nodak.edu

Natural History of Genes

http://raven.umnh.utah.edu

Access Excellence (biology)

http://www.gene.com:80/ae

Chapter Twenty-three

Professional Associations Providing Curricular Materials

Association for Supervision and Curriculum Development
1250 N. Pitt Street
Alexandria, VA 22314-1403
Tel: 703-549-9110
Fax: 703-549-3891

National Art Education Association
1916 Association Dr.
Reston, VA 22091-1590
Tel: 703-860-8000

National Association for the Education of Young Children
1509 16th Street, NW
Washington, DC 20036-1426
Tel: 800-424-2460
Fax: 202-328-1846

National Council for the Social Studies
3501 Newark Street, NW
Washington, DC 20016
Tel: 202-966-7840

National Council of Teachers of English
1111 W. Kenyon Road
Urbana, IL 61801-1096
Tel: 800-369-6283
Fax: 217-328-9645

National Council of Teachers of Mathematics
1906 Association Drive
Reston, VA 22091-1593
Tel: 800-235-7566
Fax: 703-476-2970

National Science Teachers Association
1840 Wilson Boulevard
Arlington, VA 22201-3000
Tel: 800-722-NSTA
Fax: 703-522-6091

The following addresses are for sponsored programs that have produced some of the curriculum standards listed above:

Center for Civic Education
5146 Douglas Fir Road
Calabasas, CA 91302-1467

Geography Education Standards Project
National Geographic Research & Exploration
1145 17th Street, NW
Washington, DC 20036-4688

National Center for History in the Schools
University of California, Los Angeles
10880 Wilshire Boulevard
Suite 761
Los Angeles, CA 90024-4108

Appendix

Guidelines for Curriculum Materials Centers

The following guidelines were developed in 1992 by an ad hoc committee of the Curriculum Materials Center Interest Group of the Academic Libraries Association of Ohio, chaired by this writer. The other committee members were Betty Cleaver (The Ohio State University), Marvin Hoffert (Mount Vernon Nazarene College), and Betty Porter (Xavier University). The committee members represented large and small institutions, public and private. After the committee developed the guidelines document, it was submitted for review and approval to the other CMC directors across Ohio. Below is the final document.

Introduction

The purpose of the Curriculum Materials Center is to support the teacher education program and other professional education programs of institutions of higher learning. Location and organization of materials will vary among the institutions.

Collection

I.   Collection Characteristics:
   A. The CMC collection shall be adequate to ensure compliance with the State Department of Education standards.
   B. The CMC collection shall be of a size and quality that will carry out the mission statement of the education department/college, especially the teacher preparation component.

C. All CMC materials shall be selected with consideration for the appropriate treatment of racial, ethnic, and cultural groups and the avoidance of gender stereotyping.

D. Collection Categories:
  1. Children's and Young Adult Trade Books
      a. A varied collection shall be available, preferably in the CMC, because of the cross use of these books with other materials.
      b. This collection shall include fiction, nonfiction, picture books, folk and fairy tales, plays, and poetry.
      c. The collection shall be of a high quality, consistent with the recommendations of the standard reviewing tools.
          i. Award-winning books (Newbery, Caldecott, Coretta Scott King awards and others) shall be added annually.
          ii. Current informational books, with a special emphasis on science, mathematics, and social studies, shall be purchased annually.
          iii. Efforts shall be made to maintain a balanced collection based on the needs of the education students.
  2. Media and Instructional Materials
      a. This collection shall contain a variety of formats, with both traditional resources and new technologies represented.
      b. Materials shall represent a range of curriculum concepts, skills, topics, and trends in preschool, elementary, and secondary school curriculums as well as exceptionalities, and professional education curriculum.
      c. This collection shall be added to annually with particular attention to new curriculum emphases and patterns and technologies.
  3. Elementary and Secondary School Textbooks
      a. This collection shall reflect the texts used in the public schools in the region and schools in which the teacher education students receive field placements.
      b. Several publishers shall be represented for each grade level in the major curriculum areas, including English, social studies, language arts, science,

mathematics, music, art, health, modern languages, and vocational education. The scope of curriculum areas may vary, however, according to the certification programs of the education unit at the institution.
   c. The collection shall be updated annually, reflecting new curriculum emphases and patterns.
   d. Textbooks which are ten years old shall be withdrawn annually unless their content is specialized and of current or historical value.
4. Professional Education Collection
   a. This shall include professional teaching materials related to curriculum development, and classroom management.
   b. Special emphasis shall be placed on materials which relate to evaluation, production, and utilization of educational media and technology, as well as other curriculum materials and the use of children's and young adult literature and textbooks.
5. Teaching Activities and Bulletin Board Books
   a. This collection shall represent all major curriculum areas.
   b. Materials shall be distributed among early childhood, elementary, secondary, and special education as dictated by education student enrollment.
   c. This collection shall be added to annually with particular attention to new curriculum emphases and patterns.
6. Reference Collection
   a. This collection shall be pertinent to the collections in pre-K through 12 school libraries and shall serve as referral for students in developing curriculum.
   b. This collection shall include materials related to teacher education, children's literature (author/illustrator biographies, reviews, bibliographies, indexes), educational media and technology (reviews, indexes, directories, bibliographies), and shall contain, but not be limited to, encyclopedias, dictionaries, atlases, almanacs, and indexes.
   c. This collection shall include access to electronic databases, both in CD-ROM and on-line formats.

7. Periodicals
    a. This collection shall include professional educa-
       tion journals which provide teaching ideas and
       review curriculum materials, educational media,
       microcomputers in education, and children's and
       young adult literature.
    b. The collection shall also provide titles for chil-
       dren and young adults as indexed in the *Chil-
       dren's Magazine Index*.
8. Curriculum Guides/Courses of Study/Units of
   Study
    a. These guides shall reflect those used in the insti-
       tution's region as well as a representative collec-
       tion from other areas.
    b. Major areas of the curriculum shall be repre-
       sented with the scope reflecting the certification
       programs of the education unit at the institution.
    c. These guides shall reflect current trends in edu-
       cation and be acquired annually.

*(See addendum for collection quantity guidelines for the
above categories)*

II. Collection Development Policy
    A. The CMC shall have a written collection development
       policy reflecting its mission of supporting the teacher
       preparation and professional education programs.
    B. The collection development policy shall be developed
       cooperatively by the CMC director and members of the
       education faculty.

III. Selection Policy
    A. The CMC shall have a written selection policy, citing
       the scope of the collection and the criteria and proce-
       dures both for the selection and the deselection of the
       collection as well as the guidelines for dealing with
       challenges.
    B. The selection policy shall be developed in conjunction
       with the education department/college.

IV. Collection Access
    Materials in the CMC shall be displayed in a manner that
    is both attractive and accessible. Shelves especially de-

signed for media materials shall be used. The entire collection shall be available to CMC users.

V. Cataloging/Classification of CMC Materials
    All resources in the CMC shall be cataloged and classified according to a nationally accepted classification scheme.

VI. Bibliographic Access and Control
    Easy access to the collection shall be provided by a paper or electronic catalog.

VII. Circulation Policy
    The CMC shall have a written circulation policy reflecting the needs of education students and faculty.

VIII. Inventory of Collection
    A system of inventory control shall be in place, with some part of the process accomplished annually.

IX. Collection Maintenance
    All CMC materials and equipment shall be regularly maintained and repaired, with systematic replacement of outdated and worn-out items.

X. Collection Promotion
    Accessibility to the CMC collection shall be enhanced through the use of brochures, guides, and bibliographies prepared by the CMC staff. This shall include promotion of new materials, equipment, and services.

XI. Equipment Accessibility
    A. Equipment in the CMC shall reflect state of the art technology in education and current practices.
    B. Equipment shall be available in sufficient numbers so that CMC users are provided access to using, viewing, and listening to collection materials.
    C. Loaning of equipment is optional and shall be controlled by a written loan policy.

Services

I. Production of Instructional Materials
    The CMC shall contain equipment and supplies for users to produce their own instructional materials.

II. Instruction in Media Production and Equipment Operation
The CMC shall have a plan and a process for instruction in production techniques and equipment use. Inservice education programs shall be devised for CMC staff, faculty, and students. Training shall include hands-on work with all the equipment and computers available in the CMC.

III. Reference Services to Collection
Reference service shall include assisting the user with location of appropriate resources and assistance in defining research problems or search strategies. Reference service shall extend to materials outside the CMC.

IV. Collection Instruction/Tours/Workshops
   A. A plan shall be in place for introducing all teacher education students and new faculty to the CMC by way of class or personal orientation tours.
   B. Faculty may schedule workshops to focus on orientation to the CMC, selection and evaluation of resources, and special curriculum areas or reference sources.
   C. The CMC shall consider bringing in outside resources, such as educational leaders and authors, to offer presentations for the education students and staff.

Management, Budget, and Support

I. Planning and Goal Setting
   A. Because of the vital role the CMC plays in the teacher education and professional education program, planning and goal setting shall be carried out jointly by the CMC director, the administrator from the unit in which the CMC is placed, and education faculty representatives.
   B. CMC goals and objectives shall be contained in a written document and be reviewed and updated on a regular basis.
   C. Goal setting shall be in compliance with these guidelines.

II. Evaluation
   A. The CMC shall devise a method for regularly evaluating its collection and services. This can be accomplished

through focus groups, surveys, questionnaires, or other methods.

B. Periodic reports shall be developed showing progress toward the stated goals and objectives.

C. Education faculty and students shall assist in the evaluation process.

III. Budget Planning

The CMC director and the administrator responsible for budgeting the unit in which the CMC is housed shall jointly plan the CMC budget.

IV. Funding Level

A. The CMC budget shall be adequate to ensure compliance with the State Department of Education standards.

B. The CMC budget shall be sufficient to meet the needs of the teacher education and professional education programs.

C. The CMC budget shall provide sufficient funds to meet the minimum CMC personnel staffing level guidelines (*see Personnel, II.*) as well as additional staff and program demands.

D. After a CMC has acquired the minimum collection of materials (*see Collection, XI.*) and equipment (*see Collection, I. and Addendum*), the annual expenditures for the collection materials and equipment shall be as follows:

Full-time Equivalent Teacher Education Enrollment	Expenditures*
Fewer than 250	$5000
250–499	$5000 for the first 250 students plus $12 per student above 250
500–999	$8000 for the first 500 students plus $12 per student above 500
1000 and above	$15000 for the first 1000 students plus $10 per student above 1000

*These expenditures are for minimum service levels. If a given CMC provides additional services, such as equipment circulation, computer lab, etc., more funds need to be allocated. If exceptional demands are made on the collection because, for example, there is intense field experience involvement by students and/or there are borrowing privileges extended to outside borrowers, additional funds shall be allocated. In other cases, the CMC may house and pay for a number of professional journals. Additional money would be required for these.

V. Funding Source
The CMC budget shall be funded as part of the unit under which the CMC is administered. This does not preclude additional funding from other units.

VI. Budget Administration
The CMC budget shall be administered by the CMC director.

Personnel

I. Director
   A. The CMC director shall have a minimum of a master's degree in library media or library science with preparation in curriculum, library and information science, management, teaching methodology, and media and technology.
   B. The CMC director shall be assigned no less than half-time to the management of the CMC.
   C. The position of director of the CMC shall carry faculty rank.
   D. The CMC director shall regularly participate in continuing education so that the CMC program reflects current trends in curriculum materials and technology.

II. Support Staff
The CMC staff shall include, in addition to the director, at least one full-time technician/assistant/clerical aid. Additional staffing, professional or clerical/technical, shall depend on the size of the CMC program (size of facility, number and scope of labs, amount of internal processing of

materials, and equipment, etc.) and teacher education enrollment.

III. Student Assistants
      Sufficient undergraduate student assistants/graduate assistants shall be provided to assure appropriate coverage of service desks, adequate shelving of materials, shelf reading, and other clerical duties.

Facilities

I.   Hours
      During the regular academic term, the CMC shall be open an appropriate number of daytime hours to meet the needs of students enrolled in day classes. In addition, the CMC is open evenings and some weekend hours to provide service for students involved in weekday field experiences and those inservice teachers enrolled in evening classes. Appropriate summer hours shall be provided to meet the needs of the summer education program.

II.   Accessibility
      A. Facilities shall be easily accessed with furnishings appropriately placed to allow for efficient traffic flow and large enough to meet the needs of the CMC program for use of materials, equipment, and production.
      B. In compliance with the Americans with Disabilities Act, special accommodations shall be made for students and staff with disabilities.

III. Size and Environment
      A. Appropriate space and seating shall be provided for large group, small group, and independent activities, with adequate lighting and acoustical treatment for public use and staff support functions.
      B. There shall be adequate work space provided for equipment maintenance and repair, storage, and the processing of CMC materials.

IV.   State Department of Education
      The CMC facility shall be adequate to ensure compliance with the State Department of Education standards.

Addendum

Collection Quantities

Children and Young Adult—4 titles for each full-time equivalent
Textbooks—5 volumes for each full-time equivalent
Media/Instructional Materials—5 titles for each full-time
   equivalent
Teaching Activities and Bulletin Board Books—4 titles for each
   full-time equivalent
Curriculum Guides/Courses of Study/Units of Study—0.5 titles
   for each full-time equivalent

Index

215

About the Author

Gary Lare is head of the Curriculum Resources Center at the University of Cincinnati and teaches courses in the College of Education. He received his B.S.Ed., M.Ed. and Ph.D. from Kent State University in Ohio. His graduate work was in the area of curriculum and instruction with an emphasis in educational media and technology. Dr. Lare has coauthored two other books also published by Scarecrow Press, *Audiovisual Equipment and Materials*, volumes I and II.